10/16

Liars, Cheats, and Creeps:

Leaving the Sociopath Behind

52 Sessions to Freedom
in a Women's Support Group

Patricia Peters Martin, Ph.D.

Renee Forte

Praise for *Liars, Cheats, and Creeps:*

Leaving the Sociopath Behind

I am inspired by these four courageous survivors of abuse who found their voices and regained control of their lives. Their stories provide a rare glimpse into the recovery process for women who endure and survive domestic abuse. My work as an advocate for survivors is reaffirmed by their bravery and resilience.

> –Laura Kovach, M.Ed., Director of Women's Center at Georgetown University, Faculty in Women's and Gender Studies Program, Georgetown University, Washington, D.C.

This powerful book sheds light on the dark truths some people would like to keep hidden. Dr. Martin brought these women together and inspired courage to overcome the darkness within their lives. So many people need to hear their powerful stories, including those who are suffering, loved ones, and professionals.

> –Dr. Lina Racicot, Director of Graduate Psychology, American International College, Springfield, MA.

Poignant, witty, and life affirming are the three words I use to identify these four strong women. Life may have thrown horrific curves their way, but together they learned lessons from which we can all benefit. Thank you!

> –C. Lee Bennett, Captain, Retired, Springfield Police Department, Domestic Violence Unit, Springfield, MA., Adjunct faculty at Westfield State University, Westfield, MA. and Bay Path University, Longmeadow, MA.

Liars, Cheats, and Creeps provides valuable insight into the benefits of group therapy for anyone who faces the challenge of a high conflict divorce with a history of an abusive relationship. Dr. Martin offers sensible, practical tools to help parents reduce conflict and survive with a new outlook, which in turn protects the well-being of their children. Women who fear divorce will find support and guidance from the members of this therapy group.

> –Attorney Mary A. Samberg, Parenting Coordinator and Guardian Ad Litem, West Springfield, MA.

AMAZING is the only word to describe these stories of four remarkable women and their journey as members of a support group. For a year they leaned on each other in an effort to put their lives on track after domestic abuse. Through the victims' stories, the authors instruct on domestic abuse, discuss what to consider, and show how to break free of abusive relationships. An empowering presentation!

> –Mary A. Socha, J.D. Family Court Attorney, West Springfield, MA., Board Member, Woman Shelter Compañeras, Holyoke, MA .

This inspiring book invites us to join group therapy sessions, and embrace the stories without judging as four troubled women seek answers and let go of the self-blaming. Dr. Martin addresses the topics of power, control, deceit, and betrayal. These are things millions of women deal with every day, but are afraid and/or embarrassed to talk about.

> –Milta Vargas, Domestic Violence Coordinator, Springfield Police Department, Springfield, MA.

NorLights Press
762 State Road 458
Bedford, IN 47421

Printed in the United States of America
ISBN: 978-0-9976834-0-0

Book design by Sammie and Vorris Dee Justesen
Cover design by Praditha Kahatapitiya

First printing, 2016

Dedication

We dedicate this book to all women who have struggled in abusive relationships and found the courage to leave the darkness and seek recovery. For those who continue living with violence, may this book help you find your way to healing.

Also by Patricia P. Martin, Ph.D.

The Other Couch

Discovering Women's Wisdom in Therapy

NorLights Press, 2015

Through the eyes of two wise and experienced therapists, *The Other Couch* explores the lives of 36 spirited women who struggle through life challenges with courage, resilience, wisdom, and commitment.

Table of Contents

Introduction

IN HER BUSY private practice as a psychologist, Dr. Patricia Martin noticed a disturbing pattern among women who were well educated, married with children, worked outside the home, and contributed to community activities. These clients came to her office hurting, angry, astonished, and embarrassed by betrayal from the men they trusted. Their outwardly successful lives imploded when confronted with their husbands' behavior, which appeared to have a pattern.

This book was written as a lifeline for women who are living with, or have lived with, men who lie, cheat, and mistreat their wives or girlfriends. Most of these men have deep seated psychological problems and they can be charming, manipulative, addicted, potentially violent, and difficult to escape from.

Dr. Martin wondered if a support group would help free her clients who felt trapped in relationships with these men. She took a risk that sharing their pain would help women heal their souls. The group became a valuable tool for healing, and this book emerged from the women's collective experience. The stories are written from the point of view of all the participants and Dr. Martin. You, the reader, have your own chair in the group, The Reader's Chair—a place to comment and ask questions.

1

Liars, Cheats, and Creeps profiles four smart, educated women with careers and families who were lied to and devastated by the men who promised to love and protect them. For such women, this book sends a clear message: You are not stupid, you are not alone, and you will most definitely survive.

If you are hurting, but can't find a support group, open this book and turn to a section that fits your needs. The episodes described by these women make the subject raw and real, accompanied by advice from a doctor of psychology to help with finding solutions in your own life.

Liars, Cheats, and Creeps is a user-friendly book and the next best thing to attending a support group led by an expert therapist in family counseling. Along with personal stories, the research data and links to resources will help you chart a course through the frightening maze of a dysfunctional relationship.

May this book help you get through another day and help you rebuild a better life.

Patricia Martin, Ph.D.
Renee Forte

Meet the Members

THE WOMEN in *Liars, Cheats and Creeps* are a composite of many women who've been in the support group. You will come to recognize their voices in this book as you journey with them through a year of group support therapy. Through this sharing I hope you'll find the strength to unchain yourself from the horror of your own personal abusive hell.

While I have changed the identifying information for the women and their family members, the episodes are, unfortunately, real. Let me describe the four brave women who will share their stories as we begin the group therapy sessions.

Debbie is a tiny dynamo with lively blue eyes who wears her blonde hair in a spiky cut. She always wears bright clothing accented by funky, dangling earrings that glitter as she moves her head. Debbie is assertive and has a no nonsense attitude when giving her opinion of what's right and wrong.

When she first entered therapy, Debbie was frazzled, frustrated, and angry with her husband. She was used to solving problems at work and hoped she could "fix" her marriage. I knew her forthright style would be valuable to the therapy group, yet I would probably have to rein her in at times so the other women could express their viewpoints.

Sharon is a contrast to Debbie—tall and willowy, with rich auburn hair. When I met Sharon for the first time I thought of the movie *Stepford Wives*, because she appeared perfect beyond belief. She takes great care of her personal appearance, covering her pale skin with exactly the right amount of blush to give her the appearance of health and well-being. Yet, she often seems worn out, and her thinness gives her an almost waifish quality. Her French tipped manicured nails, always without a chip; her perfectly styled hair, designer clothes, and expensive jewelry gave her the air of a trophy wife. I rarely saw Sharon wear the same article of clothing twice during the year we met for individual therapy. The contrast between her put-together look and the chaos she described in her life was striking. I noticed her deep brown eyes often had a deer-in-the-headlights expression. Rarely smiling, she typically sat in the corner of the office loveseat with a pillow hugged tightly to her chest. Sharon is slow to speak and when she does, her voice is soft and low. I hoped she would find her voice in the support group.

Then there's **Stephanie**, a physically fit, curvy woman who enjoys showing off her physical assets. She often wears tight fitting tops to show her ample cleavage, along with designer jeans tucked into spiky heeled boots. Stephanie stands about five feet nine inches tall—the perfect height for a fashion model. She has amazing hazel green eyes and long, wavy light brown hair with blond highlights.

Stephanie gives herself a weekly self-manicure to express her mood of the week. When she feels good about herself the nails are bright pink, while on other therapy visits they are black and Goth looking to reflect her dark emotions.

Stephanie has a throaty voice, a hearty laugh, and a sharp, sarcastic wit. She can swear with the best of them when need be, and then be gentle and kind in the next breath.

Stephanie loves funky jewelry from the local second-hand store where she finds most of her clothing. She's usually tanned from taking long, fast outdoor walks to burn off steam. When she arrives in sneakers instead of boots, I always know we'll have an intense session.

Street-smart Stephanie taught me practical wisdom during our sessions, and I predicted her common sense approach to life would be a valuable asset to our support group.

4

Renee was the fourth group member, a woman of wisdom and grace with a quiet, serene personality. She dressed simply, usually wearing black, white, and grey. "It's easier that way" she once told me. Renee frequently accessorized with scarves in defiance of her ex-husband, who mocked her for wearing them. She wore comfortable, yet stylish, shoes and tortoise rimmed glasses that flattered her oval face. Her light brown hair was styled in a simple shoulder length cut. I discovered that Renee's softness could change quickly when something morally repugnant provoked her. She was an excellent listener and a deep thinker, often bringing articles to her individual sessions for us to talk about.

I would describe Renee as "still waters running deep." She entered individual therapy several years before the group began, right after she first consulted a lawyer about ending her marriage. At that time Renee was distraught, distracted, and—to put it mildly, a mess. Her original disheveled appearance slowly changed to one of calm and order, even though she still felt tense and upset at times. As we began the support group, years had passed since Renee began therapy and I felt certain she'd bring sound words of wisdom to the group members.

You, the reader, are the final group member. I like to think you chose this book to help you or someone you care about survive and reclaim a disrupted life. You will be sitting in the room with us during each session, so you can feel love and support from the group members. We are delighted to have you with us.

If you met these four women at a social event, you'd never think they were dealing with conniving and violent husbands. To the outside world they appear competent and collected. That is the mask they wear to survive. Many of us wear such a mask. But in the privacy and security of my office and the support group, they can fall apart and ask for help. They can reveal their true selves. Welcome to our support group—a place of safety and truth telling.

Session One

Getting Acquainted

Pat: Hello, everyone. It's so wonderful to see you all here tonight! As Humphrey Bogart said in the movie *Casablanca*, "This could be the beginning of a beautiful friendship."

In any case, you're here to share and help each other with the strains and stresses of your lives, both now and in the past. Tonight, rather than getting into the gory details of your lives, let's use this first session to meet one another and share a bit about yourselves, so we can get to know one another simply as women, not just women in abusive relationships. In future sessions we'll dig into the nitty-gritty of your lousy relationships. Tonight we get acquainted.

I know you're each familiar with me as your individual psychologist, but tonight I'm part of your support group. I've been married 37 years to my college sweetheart, Jim. We have four grown children and three grandchildren. I've been a psychologist for 30 years now and I love what I do. In my spare time I like to write, paint, and play racket sports. I also like to attend plays and movies, and I'm a fan of college basketball. I enjoy working out in gym classes and I've been practicing yoga for 20 years. I also love to travel. So that's me!

Renee: Hi everyone. My name is Renee. I'm 59 years old, with four grown children. I was married for 28 years until my divorce about three years ago. My ex-husband is a terrible person and my divorce was . . .

Pat: Not yet, Renee. Talk about yourself. What are your interests? Tell us about your career.

Renee: Well, I worked most of my career in a good job as a tax preparer for a national company. I have four children ranging in age from 21 to 29. I worked part time while raising the kids, then full time when the youngest started in middle school. The stress from my divorce made it hard to concentrate, so I needed to retire from the company about two years ago. Now I'm doing individual tax prep work so I can work from home.

Um, what are my interests? Honestly, my biggest interest is getting better. The only other stuff I can think of is that I belong to a book group and volunteer at a soup kitchen. Once a month is all I can handle. I used to love to cook and go to movies and concerts, but now I pretty much just visit with my sisters and a couple of friends in the neighborhood.

Pat: Thanks, Renee. How about you, Stephanie?

Stephanie: Hello everyone, I'm Stephanie. I'm 46, and on the verge of getting a divorce. I swear, one more insult slung my way, and I'm gonna jump. I was a stay at home mom when my kids were little. I have two boys. Now they're teenagers, and some days they also make me want to jump off a cliff.

Pat: How about your interests?

Stephanie: Well, I have a college degree with a major in sociology, but you wouldn't know it now to look at me. I'm now working in the floral department of a Stop and Shop supermarket. Yeah, big deal. I used to do a lot in the community, like the PTO—I was the president, and I led a story time at the library, which I absolutely loved. I worked on lots of events for little league. Crap. I'm talking in the past tense like I'm dead.

Pat: You're here now, and very much alive. In fact, weren't you telling me recently about a race at the high school?

Stephanie: Right. I belong to the parents' booster club at the local high school. We have a blast raising money and going to the games. Last weekend we had a race of just parents, so a lot of people were gasping for air and barely made it to the finish line. I came in second. I ran track in high school. We also recently went with the team to a Revolution game. That's the pro soccer team. My sons both play soccer and baseball, and my sister and I are their biggest and noisiest fans.

Pat: Thanks, Steph. Sharon, will you give us an update about yourself?

Sharon: Hi. I'm Sharon, and I'm 42 years old. I've been married for nine years. I have a seven year old son and a five year old daughter. My husband is a top executive with a pharmaceutical company. He's often away on business. Those are the good days. I have a journalism degree from NYU, and I worked in publishing after college. I don't work outside the home now. When we moved to this area I was busy decorating the house and getting to know our new community. I love being a mom and I love where I live, but my marriage is awful. My husband scares me. I'm here tonight because Pat says you'll understand my situation and that I'm not alone in this kind of marriage.

Pat: Can you tell us about your interests, Sharon?

Sharon: I can't think of anything. I don't have any hobbies, unless you call shopping a hobby. Taking care of my kids is my job and my life.

Stephanie: I can't help noticing those great boots you have on, Sharon.

Sharon: Thank you. I got them in New York. I love to shop in New York City.

Stephanie: That's a great outfit, too.

Sharon: Thanks for saying that, because I really feel like I look awful. I didn't sleep well last night. I sleep poorly most nights—I'm almost too tired to sleep. I used to work out three times a week at a fitness class and I played tennis on Saturdays. Now, I just want to put my head down on this pillow.

Debbie: Who's with your kids now when you're here?

Sharon: My mom is visiting. My husband is out of town, which is why I can come here tonight. Actually he's in Germany for a week. It's easier for me to do things when he's away.

Pat: I'm glad you could make it here tonight, Sharon. Okay, Debbie, your turn. Tell us about yourself.

Debbie: I'm Debbie and I married a drunk. How's that for an intro?

Pat: For tonight let's not talk about him. Okay? Talk about you.

Debbie: Okay, I'm 57. I have two kids, was married for twenty years, and got a divorce almost three years ago. But I'm in court all the time so I feel like I am still divorcing. Before we got married I worked for a hotel in administration, and I continued that job for many years after we married. I love the hospitality business. It's always changing, and there's some traveling too, which I love, especially to resorts for conventions. During most of our marriage I was the primary bread-winner in our family. I also owned a restaurant with my husband. That was his job, managing our restaurant. We have two daughters. They were in daycare and had babysitters when they were young. Then school.

Pat: Other than work, what are your interests, Debbie?

Debbie: Well, suing my ex-husband and working and trying to get my daughters into college take up most of my time. Oh, I made these earrings. I make jewelry at night when I'm watching TV. I have to keep busy or I'll lose my mind.

Renee: They're beautiful. Do you sell the jewelry you make?

Debbie: No, but I give a lot as gifts. I was thinking about having a table at our church craft fair. Maybe I'll launch a business when things settle down. That reminds me, I do things at my church—like organize the crafts fair, the church picnic, and I'm in charge of decorating the church for Christmas and Easter.

Pat: Thank you for telling us about yourselves tonight. You are all amazing women and I think you can help each other by sharing your stories in the sessions to come. See you next week!

Reader: Hi, I'm the Reader. I'm sitting in with these sessions, hoping to learn something from this group of women and Dr. Martin. I'm trying to figure out my life before it's too late.

The Nightmare Begins

Session Two

He Betrayed Me and I Hate Him

Pat: Why don't we begin by having each of you describe what brought you to therapy? Renee, will you start?

Renee: My husband gave me gonorrhea.

Debbie: How horrible, Renee. How did you find out?

Renee: One night in April about seven years ago, my husband came home from work. It was nine o'clock and I was sitting at my computer checking emails. My daughter, Elizabeth, had gone to bed minutes before. Bob seemed nervous, so I wondered what was up. I turned away from the computer and looked up at him.

"You need to see a doctor and get checked for gonorrhea." He dropped this bombshell in a normal voice, like he was telling me we needed milk from the store. It took me a few seconds to process what he meant, and then I slid out of my chair and fell to the floor with my heart pounding so hard I couldn't hear anything.

13

"How did this happen?" I finally managed to ask him.

He told me he'd been with a prostitute when he went out with a client and got drunk, but it was only one time. Like doing it just once made everything okay.

I locked him out of the bedroom and spent a horrible night thinking about what this meant for our marriage, our family, and for me. I felt like something awful—a disease—had entered my body—something he got from another woman and then brought home. I was faithful to him for 27 years, and suddenly I could have gonorrhea from a woman he bought on the street.

It was humiliating, but I had to see a gynecologist and get tested. The test was positive. I cried in the doctor's office, but he was great. He'd delivered all four of my children, and now this! The doctor told me I should find a good divorce attorney. How humiliating is that?

So I asked around and made an appointment with a lawyer. She told me to get a grip so I could make decisions during the divorce process. I was a mess in her office, and she said I needed to get counseling right away.

Stephanie: Are you okay now?

Renee: Well, I don't have gonorrhea anymore, but whether I'm okay is complicated. For the gonorrhea, my doctor had to prescribe a strong new antibiotic because gonorrhea has become resistant. I also had to be tested multiple times for HIV. I felt disgusting. As things got worse, I lost a lot of weight, had panic attacks, post-traumatic stress, and even my hair was falling out. I'm better now after treatment, but I still have stomach problems, migraines, fibromyalgia, and trouble sleeping. And my kids are suffering too. So, I'm not really okay, but I'm working on it with Pat.

Pat: Stephanie, what brought you to therapy?

Stephanie: My husband has been drinking more and more, and getting more violent along with the alcohol use. He yells and shoves me around when he gets angry. The biggest incident was when he hit me and choked me. We'd been having trouble for a few years, but his violence was the last straw. I was able to get out of the house and I called my sister on my cell. I met her at a friend's house on my street. They both told me I had to get a restraining order and a divorce. I filed a restraining order and we're separated, but I haven't decided yet if the marriage is over. There were a lot of insults and shouting and some roughness before this. He called me every name in the book. Everyone keeps telling me I have to get out of the marriage, but I don't know what I'll do.

Sharon: My husband is getting violent too. He followed me into the garage one day and threw me against the wall. He yelled about how terrible I was as a wife and a mother. I don't even know what set him off. He wasn't like this when we married nine years ago, but now he's getting very controlling, and he got violent that day. He shoves me to get out of his way all the time. I talked to a divorce lawyer once, and I'm in therapy with Pat. I'm still thinking about what to do.

Stephanie: It sounds like we have the same husband.

Sharon: Yes, it does. But I'm not sure I'm even ready to leave him, because I have two small children: my son is seven and my daughter is five years old. My husband is an executive at a big pharmaceutical company. I don't work outside the home and I don't have much savings. I have a lot to consider.

Pat: I agree you both have a lot to think about, Sharon and Stephanie. I hope the group will help you get clarity on what is abuse and help you find the strength to decide what's in your best interests for the future. What about you, Debbie?

Debbie: My situation is complicated, at least for me. I call my husband Cheater, because that's exactly what he is. We were married for 23 years. My daughters are now 20 and 17. I thought our troubles were behind us when my husband stopped drinking after I first threatened to leave him. The kids were about eight and five, so that was a long time ago. But about five or six years ago he started being home less and less.

I had a feeling something was wrong, so I hired a private investigator. I was worried about him drinking again or gambling. The PI found out my husband was not only drinking again, but also sneaking around with a woman who worked at a massage parlor and had been investigated for neglecting her own children. When I confronted him, he said he was confused about what he wanted. I tried to keep the marriage together, but he cheated again and again. I hate to admit it, but I didn't want to get divorced. My husband filed for divorce while I was getting ready to divorce him. We spent more than two years getting through the process, because we had a restaurant business together. Now, three years later, Cheater has violated the divorce decree many times. He isn't paying the alimony or child support. I'm back in court all the time. His lawyer is awful and lies to protect him.

Sharon: I don't know if my husband ever cheated on me. He travels a lot for his job, but I don't think he's been with other women. He does drink too much. I don't hate my husband. I don't love him either. What I hate is when he gets angry. And if I asked for a divorce, he would be very, very angry. I'm just numb.

Stephanie: I don't know if my husband has been unfaithful. I know his voice makes me cringe. He's always yelling, calling me names, and telling me I can't do anything right. I don't want to be around him when he's drinking. Now, since he moved in with his brother, he keeps insulting me in text messages. I really don't know how to make him stop. I need time to think. I don't want to hate him, because he's my children's father. I just don't want him near me. I don't want to hear his voice.

Renee: I know I do hate my ex. A couple of weeks after that horrible night when he told me he'd been with a prostitute, I suddenly realized this wasn't the only time he was unfaithful. I wanted the truth. So one night I stayed up late until he got home.

Debbie: He still lived at home?

Renee: Yeah. He moved out at the first of the next month. Before he moved out, he would creep back home only when he thought we were all asleep. He was staying in my son's old bedroom.

One night while I waited for him to get home, my thoughts got messed up. I went outside in the pitch dark and lay down in the driveway so he'd run over me in his car when he got home.

Debbie: Why would you do that? He was the guilty creep, not you.

Renee: I felt worthless, and I wanted to stop that feeling. I thought he should just finish me off.

Debbie: What happened then?

Renee: One good thought got through my brain somehow: my kids. My daughter was sleeping upstairs. My other kids were off on their own by then, and I loved them all. I loved them so much. So I got up, went back inside, and waited in the kitchen to confront him—alive—when he finally came home. He finally drove up some time after midnight and came in the kitchen door. I sat on the floor just inside the door. He sat in a chair and stared at the floor while I asked questions. He finally admitted he'd been with other women since the birth of our first child, starting with people at work, including a summer delivery girl—a teenager! He also admitted he'd been seeing prostitutes for a long time.

I didn't even cry then. I think I went numb. This could not be happening. I couldn't picture my husband, an accountant in a suit, approaching a prostitute on the street. I asked him if he wore a disguise. He said no, and actually explained his procedure for buying sex on the street, and how he would make sure the woman wasn't a cop. I felt like I was in a horror movie. I could hardly believe this was me, in our kitchen, with the husband I trusted.

He seemed to enjoy going into detail about how much certain sex acts cost and where he would go to have sex, which was usually not far from where we lived. He was actually bragging about his own cleverness. He was smirking! It seemed like he enjoyed shocking and hurting me.

Somehow I managed to ask how many times he was with prostitutes: three times, four times? He told me he had sex with "sex workers" (his term) about 650 times over the last 25 or 26 years—often on the way to or from work, and sometimes at lunchtime. He actually told me the working girls thought he was a good customer. Then he asked me, "Can you believe I paid for sex?" I think he took great pleasure in telling me every sordid detail.

My brain was trying to slam the door on his words. I could not breathe. By then I was sobbing. I called my sister, at 3 a.m., and she cried with me. I really don't know how I functioned after that.

Debbie: How disgusting! Did he show any sign of caring about how you felt?

Renee: No, not at all. All he said at the end was that he didn't plan on telling me anything, but I insisted. So in his mind, I asked for it. After our conversation he just wandered into the family room and turned on the TV. Somehow I got up the stairs to call my sister. She got me through that night.

I had no idea he was unfaithful even once. Instead, he was never faithful. My entire married life was a fraud. This was a complete betrayal of me, our marriage, our children, everything. Every day of 27 years was a lie. He would tell us he had to work late and on weekends for our family. Lies! He lied to me and our children that he was a man who loved and protected us. The life I thought we had was an illusion. I hate him, and I've never hated anyone before.

Debbie: I hate Cheater too, and it makes me furious. My kids feel betrayed and rejected. He threw us all away like garbage for his massage parlor whore.

Stephanie: In the beginning of our marriage, my husband was considerate, affectionate, and generous. Occasionally he had hissy fits, as I called them. But over the last few years, he's become more violent and angry. I didn't see the changes for a long time because they were gradual. It's amazing what you can get used to over time. Now I feel I was tricked and betrayed by him, because he's a different man. He whittled away at me over time and undermined my values, self-esteem, and my standards for myself and how I wanted to raise my family. I can't believe this is happening. I hate my life.

Renee: I hate that I hate my ex. It makes me hate him even more that he pushed me down this far. Is it wrong to have this feeling?

Pat: All your emotions are understandable and normal. You are all in pain. Your husbands have betrayed your trust and your lives are upended. My goal in counseling is to help you understand what kind of men these are and eventually help you detach from them to the point they seem like annoying bugs you can swat away. But, this will take time. Right now, anger and hatred are still there. Don't add to your problems by feeling guilty about your feelings. You won't feel this way forever. Please try and take care of yourselves now. Don't drink and drive, and be careful. Stress can make you forgetful and clumsy, and I know you're all under enormous stress. Do whatever you need to stay healthy.

Stephanie: Healthy? I'm just trying to survive every day.

Pat: You will survive. We're here to help you. Please try to eat healthy food, take time to exercise—even for just for ten minutes a day—and try to get decent sleep. If you take good care of yourselves, you'll all get through this with help from the group and individual therapy. Remember, you are amazing, resilient women!

Reader: These women were betrayed by men who promised to love, honor and cherish them. This happens so often, it isn't even news. It makes me wonder what is normal.

Not As You Think

You say I should be ashamed
because you degrade me;
You say I embarrass you.
You think you can step on me

Did you shame her? How much did she cost you?
Did you degrade her? Did you see her desperation?
Did you embarrass her?
Did you step on her?

I am ashamed you are my husband.
You degrade yourself.
You embarrass the human race.
Get out of my way.
You feel no shame.

–Renee

Session Three

What is Normal?

Pat: Let's pick up where we left off last time. What became "normal" for you that you now see was not normal?

Debbie: I don't think cheating in a marriage is normal, or at least I don't want to think it is. But it seems awfully common in our society. Cheater actually shouted at me once, "All men cheat on their wives!" If you read the tabloids, go to movies, or watch daytime television, every day we hear about more politicians and celebrities cheating on their wives.

Pat: Not all men cheat on their wives. Debbie and Renee, you know your husbands cheated. We don't know about Sharon or Stephanie's husbands. In any event, your ex-husband is incorrect, Debbie. Not all men cheat. Many good men are disgusted by the idea. Decent men do exist, but you need to be aware that some people—men and women—live without a moral code. They believe they have the right to do whatever feels good to them, regardless of how it affects others, including their wives and families.

Renee: Hearing about these scoundrels upsets me. I never paid much attention to scandals in the news until I figured out I'd married a scoundrel myself.

Debbie: I always thought all the cheating we hear about in the news happened to other people. Never in my home. Now, I realize it's all around me and even infected my own family. This has totally changed how I see the world.

Renee: You asked about normal, Pat? My marriage wasn't typical, or what I think is typical for other people, but it seemed normal to me. My ex worked all the time, but I did tax prep work, and I knew about the long hours, especially before April 15. Sometimes I brought work home and worked for two or three hours after the kids went to bed. My ex had a successful accounting practice and that meant new work came in all the time. I understood and accepted that he worked late at night and on most weekends.

Stephanie: When was he home?

Renee: His normal day was to get up after everyone left for school or work, and come home after the kids went to bed. He'd make himself dinner or bring home take out. Then he watched TV and often fell asleep on the couch. He was home with the family on Saturdays. He also went to the kids' games and performances, and even coached a beginner's soccer team one season.

I didn't complain or nag about his absence from our daily lives. I thought I was being a flexible, modern woman. He wasn't around a lot; he was the main bread winner and I was the main parent, and when I worked full time I had help from a reliable older woman who came to the house every day. So that became our "normal." I had no idea what he was doing all those years. He told me he was working, and I believed him.

Debbie: Once Cheater stopped drinking, I thought our lives were pretty normal. He worked a lot at the restaurant. I did the books at home and still consulted with the hotel, so we seemed like a good team. I was shocked when I found out he was going to sex shop massage parlors, and even more devastated when I learned he wanted to live with one of the hookers. I kept thinking this was a midlife crisis and he'd wake up one day. That day never came.

Stephanie: Normal for me was getting the kids off to school and trying to keep the house picked up and nice for my husband before I went to my part time job. He would continually complain and yell at me that I was a slob and white trash. Our house was never clean enough for him. He came from a wealthy family and acted like he was my savior. He made me think I was lucky to catch him. Over time, normal became making sure I took care of everything, so nothing would set him off. Every day I checked in with him at work to see what kind of day he had and what mood he was in before he got home, so I could prepare. This became normal to me over time. I'm not sure how it happened that I learned to put up with that way of life. Everything was so gradual. I never imagined I'd turn out to be one of those women, but I did. I just didn't realize what was happening. The excuses became rationalizations in my own mind, and it fed my need to nurture. I wanted to make things better for my family, and he took advantage of that with his manipulative logic.

Debbie: Same with me. In my mind, keeping the family happy and together was my goal. So I kept trying time after time to keep making things "normal," taking care of the house and the kids, trying to please him.

Stephanie: Every day before we separated, he griped about all the stress at work, which excused his behavior to me. I tried to make everything perfect and not stressful for him. That gave me the feeling of making a difference, and I convinced myself if I could only be better and do better, he wouldn't have to get angry. I told myself, "This man loves me, so he has my best interests at heart." He always twisted things around so I was responsible for his angry outbursts and abuse. And that reminds me now of a joke he used to tell: "What does every abused woman have in common? Get ready, here comes the punchline: They just don't listen."

He always laughed at his own jokes, but somehow I missed the humor in that situation.

Renee: When did you start seeing things differently?

Stephanie: Even before the choking episode I was beginning to view him in a different light. I think it started when I watched Charlie Sheen's manic rants on TV and YouTube and saw how the rest of the world reacted to behavior that seemed normal to me. My friends and family called to ask if I'd heard Charlie Sheen. My sister was the most persistent. She told me to listen and tell her what I heard. She said, "He sounds just like your husband. Pay attention to how other people react to it."

I did listen, but I couldn't understand why everyone was so upset. Charlie's behavior didn't offend me or even make my mouth drop open. After all, he hadn't used the foul language my husband commonly used with me, so it was pretty tame from my perspective. That could be any night of the week in my house, depending on my husband's mood—and he could be a lot more aggressive than Charlie Sheen. I made a joke that my husband could teach Charlie a thing or two about vulgar and demeaning speech. I truly didn't understand what all the fuss was about.

My sister was horrified by my response. She looked me in the face and told me how sad it was that I'd become blind to my husband's disrespectful behavior. "The world is not wrong" she said. "Listen to how disgusted people are at Charlie Sheen's behavior. People around you see your husband the same way. It isn't right for you to accept this as a normal part of everyday life!"

Sharon: Hearing all of you makes me realize I'm living with an abuser. My husband puts me down all the time, plus he constantly checks on me. I kept telling myself his outbursts and controlling behavior are normal because he's the one earning the money. I thought he was just worried about me, but now I see I'm like his puppet and plaything instead of an equal partner. I'm getting fed up with this life.

Pat: The men you see behaving this way on television and in the tabloids are not normal. You've all lost sight of what is healthy and right because you were with men who constantly whittled away at your self-esteem. You began walking on eggshells to try and please your husbands, to the point of losing your own sense of value, your own sense of right and wrong. You began to accept unacceptable behavior as a way of protecting yourself, because you couldn't see any way out. With the support of this group and by removing yourself from your marriages, you'll begin to rebuild your lives as healthy and normal.

Reader: I can sense a tremendous amount of frustration and pain in this room. But it feels right to release the pain and clean it out.

Session Four

It Hurts!

The Battered Woman Syndrome, With or Without Physical Injury

Pat: Last session, we talked about how to define normal, especially in light of what we see in the media every day. You each shared how a person can get used to being treated badly. It's great that you could be honest with each other and share those thoughts and feelings. You seem upset, Stephanie. What's happening with you?

Stephanie: About fifteen minutes ago I got a text from my husband, telling me he can't pick up our son at baseball practice. I texted back a reminder that he agreed to do this because I have support group. Look at his answer from just a minute ago: "Stop ordering me around, b----. You wanted a separation, so you pick up your kids. You made your bed." And he backed that up with a horrible voicemail.

Pat: That's awful, Stephanie. He's obviously trying to block you from getting support here tonight.

Sharon: What are you going to do?

Stephanie: I'm going to call my son Jay, who's sixteen, and tell him to call his father directly and arrange the ride. I can't stand this. I'm sick of being called names. I thought the separation would stop it, but if anything, he's getting worse.

Debbie: What does he call you?

Stephanie: Every obscene name you can think of, and some you've probably never heard. He says, "You think you're so smart. Well you're not. You're a stupid b ----." He used to call me a stupid b----- when the slightest thing went wrong. I would stand up for myself at first, but that only made things worse. I soon learned that if I didn't give in, he'd get the kids involved. They were his most powerful weapon against me. He knew I'd give in and shut my mouth to protect them. Most of the time I didn't even know what might set him off. I tried to keep everything perfect, and eventually I started viewing it as a personal failure when he found something to yell about. It could be anything—we ran out of beer, dinner was hamburgers again, our son didn't have the right shin guards for soccer practice, a bill was late, it was raining outside—anything and everything was my fault. And, oh, the dread if anything broke or needed repair that I couldn't fix myself and had to tell him about. He'd shout that I just didn't respect the home he gave me to live in. This could be over a tiny thing, like forgetting to wind the cord of the vacuum cleaner the right way and just looping it around the hook.

Renee: So he talks that way in front of your kids?

Stephanie: Yes, all the time. And if I leave the room he just shouts louder. He can explain his anger and behavior to my kids so it sounds like the calmest person in the world would be driven to madness having to deal with me.

Renee: He's trying to make your kids into weapons against you.

Stephanie: Yes, and he uses them to put me down. The kids don't want their friends to come over and they spend most of their time at school, practice, or friends' houses. My husband slams doors and screeches out of the driveway in his car. He goes to his favorite bar, comes home drunk, and falls asleep in his chair. He goes to the bar almost every day on his way home from work. Once I asked him where he was when he came home

26

really late. He said he was at the bar—where else would he go when all he had at home was a stupid b----? If I cried, he'd say "Oh, the b---- is crying now. Boo hoo."

Debbie: Did you ever go to marriage counseling?

Stephanie: The first time we were separated, he actually suggested counseling. This was about 18 months ago. In the past when I mentioned counseling he acted like I was crazy to even ask. But when I mentioned getting a divorce, he said maybe we should go to a marriage counselor. We went for the three months we were separated and I truly thought he was making progress. He admitted some difficult things about his behavior and seemed genuinely remorseful. I knew I had a lot of work to do as well, being defined as submissive and co-dependent, but at the time I felt optimistic. He moved back home and things were better for a few months. I finally had the man I fell in love with; the man I thought I married.

Then his anger surfaced again, along with the drinking and drugs. His awful behavior started all over. When I took issue with this relapse, he yelled at me for holding him to "my highfalutin' standards." When I suggested we go back for more counseling, he told me therapy was bullshit, everything was my fault, and he only did therapy in order to get back into the house. Yet I still felt I loved this man. I told myself he didn't mean it—he just inflicted hurt when he was drunk and angry. Sometimes I think everything really is my fault. Maybe he's right. Like he says, maybe I just provoke his anger so I can play the victim and feel sorry for myself.

Debbie: You shouldn't believe that for one second. I think he's just manipulating you. How much of his abuse is related to his drinking?

Stephanie: Quite a lot, I think. It used to be that one or two beers made him relax. He was quiet, and he could be nice. We could watch a comedy show on TV together and laugh. That was years ago. Now he drinks a lot, and he also smokes pot. And he's mean. Really vicious. After he attacked me in the kitchen, he moved out again. Since I got the restraining order he's been texting his meanness.

Pat: What about you, Debbie?

Debbie: Cheater had a big drinking problem early in our marriage, and he was a mean drunk too. I told him I'd leave if he didn't stop. I gave him one chance and he quit, so I thought "Wow, he must really love me." After a few years, I became suspicious. He was physically and emotionally absent. He acted like everything irritated him. He was not a nice person, and didn't take much interest in the kids. At the time I knew nothing about being a dry drunk.

Stephanie: What's that?

Pat: A dry drunk is an alcoholic who stopped drinking, but has the same negative behavior he had while drinking, plus he's angry and miserable about it. A dry drunk doesn't attend Alcoholics Anonymous meetings and go through the 12 Step Program. So, he may stop drinking, but he keeps all the behaviors and moods of active drinking—angry, unhappy, and often taking frustration out on the family.

Stephanie: So if my husband stopped drinking, he might still be horrible?

Pat and Debbie: Yes!

Pat: If someone stops drinking, is an active participant in AA meetings, gets a sponsor, and works on the 12 Steps, he or she can become truly sober and healthy. I often see inspirational changes in recovering alcoholics' attitudes and how they live their daily lives. But an alcoholic who stops drinking and doesn't get emotional/psychological help often becomes a nasty dry drunk.

Stephanie: Should I get a divorce?

Pat: Stephanie, we can't tell you what to do, but we'll support whatever you decide. From what you say, your husband doesn't believe he has a drinking problem and sees no need to stop. If he did take the first step of admitting he's an alcoholic, then asked for help and attended AA meetings, maybe you'd have a chance for a better marriage. Family members should also attend Al-Anon meetings. These meetings help you understand your behavior toward the alcoholic. But without the commitment on his part, nothing will change.

Sharon, does your husband drink or do drugs?

Sharon: As far as I know he only drinks socially, though he does a lot of socializing with clients. I would be shocked if he did any drugs, because he wouldn't risk his job. My husband is unbelievably controlling and uptight.

Pat: How so?

Sharon: If we're going out with a client he tells me what to wear, and it's always a low cut, slinky outfit so he can show me off like a prize possession. He tells me what clothes to buy for the kids and what they should wear when we go to the club. If he's home for dinner he tells me what to make. He organizes all the food and dishes in the kitchen, even where stuff goes in the refrigerator. He gets mad if anything's out of place. He has complete control over the money, and every time a bill comes I have to sit and listen while he complains I'm using too much water and wasting electricity. He even checks on my phone calls. If I go out, he wants to know exactly where. He plans all our vacations without asking me what I want to do. He treats me like a child. And now, he shoves me around saying, "Get out of my way" instead of "excuse me" when he walks past. Then there was that horrible time in the garage.

Pat: Any other violence?

Sharon: Well, once he shoved me out of the car when we were driving home from a dinner party.

Debbie: What?! Was it moving?

Sharon: Yes. He was turning down our street and complaining about something I said. I got some scrapes and I walked the short distance home. Oh, and once he shoved me out the back door of our house into the snow while I was in my pajamas.

Debbie: Sharon! Why?

Sharon: He didn't like what I was saying. He says I make him crazy and he's already under a lot of pressure at work.

Pat: Work pressure is no excuse for calling you names, pushing you around, and shoving you out of cars and your own house.

Sharon: I know, I know.

Pat: How does it sound to you when you say these things out loud?

Sharon: Terrible. It sounds worse when I talk about it.

Pat: Or maybe you hear the stark reality from your own voice.

Renee, what about your ex-husband?

Renee: Well, some of this sounds familiar. I also thought the pressure my ex was under at work made him moody and curt with me. I never knew what kind of person he'd be when he came through the door after work. I learned to let him make the opening remark so I could figure out whether to stay around and chat or slip off to another room. At the beginning of our marriage we would talk a lot, cook together, and go out. He could be thoughtful and kind. After I had our first child, he worked more and we went out less. I loved being home with my kids, but he started chipping away at me. He was critical of my clothes (I dressed too Catholic), my housekeeping, my religion, my grocery shopping, my gardening, and even my driving. Anything that went wrong with the kids or the house was my fault. He even told me I made too much noise when I closed the car door.

Because he wouldn't eat the meals I fixed, we usually ate at home as a family only on Saturdays. He was always the last one to the dinner table. When I cooked, he pushed the food around his plate and then got up after dinner and emptied his plate in the garbage. Mealtime was tense, especially with four kids at the table. I tried all kinds of meals and made an effort to distract the kids from their father with talk of school and activities. By the time the kids were in high school, I stopped cooking when he was home to avoid his criticism. He either cooked for himself or ate out.

Pat: What about money, Renee?

Renee: Money always turned into a minefield for me. He first told me to use the debit card for household things. So I did, and then he'd yell and tell me I should be using the credit card. So I did, and then he'd yell and tell me I should always pay cash. He used every opportunity to call me wasteful, especially with food, like how much I spent at the grocery store. We had a good income so this was not really about money. He would pull things out of the garbage if he saw me throw out leftovers, stale bread, or an over ripe tomato. I adjusted my schedule so I never had to cook, clean, or bring groceries into the house while he was home. All this avoidance gradually increased over time.

Pat: What else?

Renee: There are hundreds of little things. Oh, here's one incident I want to share. I took up gardening when the kids stopped playing in the backyard. I took down the swing set and the sand box, made flower beds, and planted bushes. I dug up the whole back lawn and reseeded it myself. I enjoyed working in the yard and felt proud when it looked nice. I used my own money so he couldn't complain. One day, instead of backing his car out of the driveway which he had done every day for years, he decided to drive onto the backyard to turn his car around. I couldn't believe it, and I ran outside and told him so. He told me to get over it, and that everyone knows driving on a lawn doesn't hurt it. He left for work and I stared at deep tire tracks over my newly planted grass.

Debbie: What a creep. I would've gone ballistic!

Renee: If I spoke up for myself at all, he'd always say: "What's your problem?" Everything was my problem, not his. Sometimes he would cringe, scrunching his shoulders when I talked, because he said he hated my accent. I'm from Boston. Of course he knew that when we were dating. Or he would correct my grammar and ignore what I was saying. He put me down for years over what I said and how I said it. I gradually learned after 20 years to not talk much around him.

Debbie: That's infuriating. But did he talk?

Renee: Oh, yeah. He talked and talked and talked. I think he loved to hear himself talk. He complained a lot about our house, our city, and our lives in general. He used to tell me he wanted to live in the woods and write books. Yet he was the one who chose this city after grad school, and he applied for and accepted the demanding job at his accounting firm. He even selected the house we lived in. Another thing: He'd say something, and then later deny saying it. If I insisted he did, he'd tell me I was crazy. That happened a lot.

Pat: Yes, Renee, you shared many of those incidents in our individual sessions. It's called gas lighting after a famous classic movie Gas

Light. In the movie, the husband tries to drive his wife crazy by denying he said or did something. In the movie, Ingrid Bergman begins to believe she's going crazy. Mental health professionals use this term when an abusive husband or wife is trying to convince a partner they're in the wrong or crazy. It's also a way of avoiding accountability.

Stephanie: Renee, did your ex call you names or hit you?

Renee: My ex didn't shout much and didn't hit me. I guess that's why I hung in there. But I felt shredded up by him if I let myself think about it. So I avoided those thoughts. When he told me about the prostitutes, I felt like he'd punched my lights out.

Pat: Each one of your husbands disrespected you and blamed you for their unhappiness. You all learned to compensate by minimizing your feelings and making adjustments and excuses to deal with their behavior. This is called codependent behavior. Let me just take a minute to talk about codependent behavior and enabling.

When you worry more about what the other person will think or do than about being your true, authentic self, you may be in a codependent relationship. When you scurry around to get the sink scrubbed and shiny before he gets home in order to avoid criticism, then you're living a life of fear to please him, instead of living in a relaxed, calm relationship. When you color your hair or wear clothes to please him, yet inside you feel sleazy, then you aren't being true to yourself.

Trying to please each other is okay, but not at the expense of your own morality, feelings, and opinions. Also, in a healthy relationship the other partner is also trying to please you. In a healthy marriage, your husband would sometimes go to the theater with you, even if he preferred a football game. In turn, you'd attend a sporting event to show your support for him. All of you bent over backwards to try and please your husbands, only to end up feeling like failures. This is common when the wife is battered physically, emotionally, or psychologically. All of you have been battered in one way or another.

Sharon: I don't like hearing I'm codependent. It sounds like I'm at fault.

Renee: It was hard for me to hear from Pat about enabling my ex-husband. That was the last thing I thought I was doing, or ever wanted to do. I thought I was being flexible and accommodating to make my marriage work. I took my marriage vows seriously. I was always told that it takes a lot of work to have a good marriage, and we should forgive and give second and third chances after an argument. We even went to a marriage counselor. But I had no idea what kind of person I was married to.

I learned from Pat that realizing I enabled a sociopath doesn't mean I'm to blame for the abuse. That would be blaming the victim! We all enabled our husbands by trying to avoid or endure the abuse or neglect that gradually got worse.

Pat: You're right, Renee. You are not to blame for your ex's behavior, but you enabled his mistreatment of you by trying again and again to make it all better. You continued until you could enable no more. That's when you realized you had to get out.

Renee: I now realize I couldn't see what was happening because I was too busy coping. I had four children and a job. My ex was, and still is, a master manipulator just like all of yours. I think we have a lot of courage to break free from master manipulators. Is that right, Pat?

Pat: Yes, you're all amazing to be here tonight talking about everything that's happened to you. Sharing your pain takes tremendous courage, and it's wonderful that you're willing to help each other change and move on. I think you've all begun to see that making excuses to others and yourself, changing your behavior to avoid your husbands' anger, and continually hoping your husbands will change is not going to work. In fact, it makes things worse. You are here now to focus on making a better life for yourselves and your children.

Reader: These men are truly horrible. Why did such smart, accomplished women stay with them?

I Am a Window

I am a window painted shut.

Your shouting grimes my glass.

Your lies smear my glass.

Your shoving cracks my glass.

My cold panes shield me still from your hurling pain,

while I look far outside for a way to get out.

But for now,

I am a window painted shut.

–Renee

Session Five

Should I Keep Trying?

Pat: You've all told the group about the terrible things your husbands did, yet a lot of time passed before each of you chose to separate or divorce. Splitting up wasn't a quick and easy decision, was it?

Stephanie: I haven't been happy for a long time, but I've let things drag on and on. I guess I keep thinking it will get better. Mostly he isn't home, so I go about my days at work and with the kids as though he doesn't exist. I get a lot of fulfillment from that. Things are okay when he's sober, but when he drinks, he gets mean. The trouble is, he drinks and smokes pot more and more. I visited a divorce lawyer after he choked and hit me. My sister and my close friend told me he'd hurt me again and I had to get a divorce. My sister called the cops and went to court with me to file a restraining order. My parents came from New Hampshire the next day to make sure he moved his clothes out. I couldn't have done this alone. I felt kind of limp.

That day was so awful, and I'm still not sure about divorce. My family is supporting me, but they're also pushing me to make a decision, and I'm not ready yet. At one point I actually told them I believed he'd

35

be so sorry he hit me that he'd come to his senses and stop drinking. I often daydream about a scene where he announces he's a changed man, he regrets the things he did, and he's going to attend AA. I dream we go on a family vacation to celebrate.

Debbie: But you can't live in a dream, Steph. Listen to me! I don't mean to sound harsh, but I waited too long and wasted too many years of my life. Cheater was a heavy drinker when our kids were little. I told him to stop, and at first he didn't. When I finally threatened to leave him, he seemed to stop drinking for about five years. But he wasn't home much. I had no idea he was going to massage parlors and doing God knows what else.

I minimized any problems we were having as a couple. If he was impatient or said something mean, I figured he was in a bad mood because of work. I was busy with our children and my bookkeeping and consulting work, so I focused on what needed to be done each day. When I first found out he cheated on me, I confronted him and he promised it would never happen again.

I believed him. I told myself I wasn't a perfect wife and I should try harder. I made his favorite dinners on his days off, and we went out more as a couple. I tried to focus on our marriage and things seemed better for a few months. But then he fell back into the old routine of being away most of the time. I dropped into the restaurant one night, all dressed up to surprise him and have dinner. He got angry and told me to leave, saying he was too busy and I needed to trust him or our marriage was over. He put it on me. I was hurt, but it also sounded reasonable at the time because he worked hard and was under pressure. So I let things slide for a while. For all I know, one of his girlfriends was at the restaurant that night.

Renee: Looking back, I wish I'd left my ex after the first unkind thing he said to me. Instead, I tried to brush things off, make everything better, or stay quiet and out of sight as a last resort. I kept trying to plan a night out or vacation that would please him, but nothing ever did. I believed I was a smart person, so I should be able to improve my marriage and change him into a caring, loving man. I thought my kids and I were good people and I just needed to try harder so he'd see how lovable we were. I convinced myself that if I remained flexible and patient, he'd begin paying attention to us and want to be with us. I tried and tried. And I believed I should try because I was married to him and he was the father of our children.

Sharon: Well, marriage does take a lot of work, doesn't it? And my husband is under stress at his job. I want him to go back to being the guy I married. People can change—right? I hate the whole idea of going through a divorce.

Pat: Sometimes a person will change, but only if he or she wants to change. Each one of you made numerous changes to try to make your marriages work, but you can't change the other person.

Reader: I would be afraid to live with any of these men. I wonder why these women find it so hard to dump their abusive husbands.

Session Six

Afraid to Leave and Afraid to Stay

Pat: Stephanie, your husband choked you and knocked you down. You must have been terrified. You also endure frequent verbal abuse. Why is it hard for you to think about divorce?

Stephanie: As awful as my husband is, I can't imagine being a divorced mother with two teenage boys at home, especially since we're struggling to pay the mortgage on our house, two car loans and all the other bills.

When he has just one drink, life isn't so bad. But he drinks more and more now. To tell you the truth, I'm afraid he'll hurt me if I decide to divorce him. He went crazy when I got the restraining order after he choked me.

Pat: What do you mean?

Stephanie: He told the kids I hit him first, which is a lie. He also told them I asked for it because I was out of control that night and throwing things. Of course, none of that is true. He's the one who throws things, like the beer can he threw against the kitchen wall that night, and the toaster he threw and nearly hit me. Now that we're separated, he still yells at me from his car at the end of the driveway. He sends abusive text messages and leaves horrible voicemail messages. He's livid because I went through with the restraining order. He tells the kids it's all my fault and I wrecked our family. Every night I'm afraid he'll get into the house and hurt me, or drive me off the road and cause an accident.

Pat: Did you change the locks?

Stephanie: Yes, but locks won't stop him. He just needs to stop being so awful. Unfortunately, he'll always be around because of the kids. So why get a divorce? It'll just make him worse.

Pat: We'll have to talk more about setting boundaries and making a safety plan to help you feel less out of control and afraid. You already have a restraining order, so you need to call the police if you ever feel threatened or he comes on your property. Have a cell phone with you at all times, and don't hesitate to dial 911 if you feel threatened or he comes near you. Try not to be alone when you go out. Your boys are teenagers now, but in a few years when they're adults you won't need to deal with your husband.

Debbie: I didn't fear my husband like you do, Stephanie, but I think I was afraid of not having a husband. I gave Cheater second chances, and he stopped drinking—or I thought he did. I told him he could never cheat on me again. He promised me he wouldn't, but he broke that promise too. I didn't fear him, but I didn't want to give up on my marriage. Maybe I was afraid of admitting I didn't have a real marriage. The divorce process is awful, and it truly was a last resort for me.

Sharon: I think I could have a happy marriage if my husband would stop being so controlling. I don't want to get a divorce unless I absolutely have to.

Pat: There's no question that divorce is unpleasant. This isn't an easy decision, but the only thing worse than divorcing an abuser is staying married to an abuser. What about you, Renee?

Renee: I sometimes thought about divorce when I was especially miserable, but mostly I tried to change the subject in my brain. You called that compartmentalizing. I'd focus only on good times we had, and those became fewer and fewer. Now I think I didn't have the courage to act before the night he dropped the gonorrhea bomb on me. We had four kids and I decided I could put up with his moods and absences in order to keep the family together. I told myself the kids needed a father, and at least he didn't beat me, so I could survive. I worked at home as a tax preparer, which didn't bring in a lot of money. I was afraid I'd end up living in my car if I filed for divorce. When the three older children left the house I hoped our marriage would improve, because life would be less hectic at home. So I stayed in the marriage, even though it didn't get better. After he broke the news that he had gonorrhea from a prostitute, I thought he might even try to kill me to try to keep me quiet. Anything was possible.

Sharon: I can think of many reasons I haven't separated and begun a divorce. I think my kids need a father, and I don't know how we'd live. If I depended on alimony, he would still control me.

Pat: You all feel trapped in a space where your options are limited. The fear you feel is caused by loss of control, but trying to control the chaos of your marriages is a mirage. The only real control we have in our lives comes from making decisions about our own behavior. You've all sought counseling, and this is a brave step. Debbie and Renee have divorced; Stephanie has separated, and Sharon is still living with her husband in the same house, trying to decide about the next step. You must all continue moving forward and have courage to make decisions in the best interests of you and your children. Serenity will come when you realize you can't control and change others, but you do have the ability to make changes in your own life. This will empower you to create a healthy life for yourself.

Reader: Divorce versus a bad marriage. Are those the only choices? And what about those *other women* who get involved with married men?

Session Seven

The Other Women

Pat: Hi, everyone. Sharon couldn't get a baby sitter, so she isn't with us tonight. Debbie, you made an interesting comment when you came in. Why don't we start with that and see where things go. Can you repeat what you said?

Debbie: I sure can. Cheater is a liar and a world class creep.

Renee: Don't hold back on our account.

Pat. What's going on with your ex?

Debbie: I saw him and his tramp girlfriend coming out of JB's Liquor Store, next to Harvest Grocery store in the little plaza. I pick up groceries there a lot.

Pat: That made you angry?

Debbie: I'm a lot more than angry—I'm absolutely furious. He's with her, buying liquor, at 2:30 in the afternoon. He's supposed to be at the restaurant. He's not taking care of the business as he's required to do under the divorce settlement. He still owes me $30,000 from the business,

43

and he's hanging out with this woman in the middle of the afternoon. Besides that, she looks pregnant. I am soooo mad.

Renee: I'd hate to bump into my ex, with or without any of his women. I just never want to see him again. Ever.

Stephanie: I'm facing the same thing right now. A friend saw my husband with a woman a couple of weeks ago. I found out she's one of the secretaries at his family's company. When I first heard about it, I was hurt. I'm in pain over our marriage and he's having fun with his secretary.

Pat: How do you feel?

Stephanie: I feel like throwing up. I'm living in survival mode, and he's already dating his secretary. What a pathetic cliché! I've met her before, of course, and she takes my calls to my husband. We haven't even filed for divorce yet. I've got to call my lawyer.

Pat: Definitely update your lawyer. For here and now, let's talk about your feelings. Debbie, your ex cheated on you while you were married, and he's now with this other woman. This must hurt you.

Debbie: He left me for a sleazy massage parlor prostitute. I went online, and his Facebook page is disgusting, with pictures of her and the two of them together.

Renee: Why did you go to his Facebook page?

Debbie: I believe knowledge is power. I need to know what he's doing to keep myself safe. I also Googled her and found out a lot about the skanky b—.

Renee: I'm the opposite. I don't want to know anything and I wish I'd never met my ex. In fact, I wish he didn't exist. I don't want him in my present or my future.

Stephanie: But how did you feel when he told you he was with hundreds of women?

Renee: When he told me how often he cheated and that it continued throughout our marriage, I was reeling. So much sewage came out of his mouth. The fact that he had sex with a teenager who worked at his office really shocked me. I actually knew another woman he cheated with, and he wanted me to guess her identity like it was a game. She works at Family Services, so they are both unbelievable hypocrites. She knew he was married, she knew me, and she knew about our four children. Yet she still felt she could help herself to my husband and dive bomb my family. I called her and told her she'd better get checked for gonorrhea and AIDS. He was standing right there trying to grab the phone away from my hand.

Pat: What are your feelings about the prostitutes?

Renee: I was shocked and appalled, of course. I went to the pastor of our church for counseling, and he was shocked and appalled too. I told him everything. Anyway, I did a lot of research and learned about addiction to porn and sex, and how narcissistic sociopaths feel they're entitled to do whatever they want. I also learned about women, girls, and boys who are trafficked to perform in porn videos and sell their bodies. About 98% of these people have been abused or neglected and either ran away from their homes or aged out of foster care. Most are addicted to drugs and desperate for money to buy their next fix. After they've been arrested they can't get regular jobs, so the future looks hopeless. When I told my ex about my research, he said he was helping his working girls because he was a good customer. Disgusting.

I've learned to refer to those women my husband bought as prostituted women, not prostitutes. They are desperate and exploited. Even the so-called high class women are shells of themselves. Human trafficking is huge and awful.

Pat: It sounds like you have pity for them.

Renee: Now I do. My ex is the terrible person, not them. Do you know what he told me about the girl he bought who gave him gonorrhea?

Stephanie: What?

Renee: He told me she was an amateur. I wanted to throw up. It took a while, but now I pray for that girl and all the other human beings he exploited and treated as objects. I now regard the girl who gave gonorrhea to him as an angel—my angel.

Stephanie: Why?

Renee: If she hadn't passed her disease through him to me, I'd still be clueless and married to that scum. So this nameless girl is my angel. I pray she is somehow having a better life now.

Stephanie: Sheesh. Do you feel that way about the cougar from Family Services?

Renee: No.

Stephanie: I don't pray for Mary the Slutty Secretary that's for sure. They're both getting exactly what they deserve, if karma has any say, and it always does. I don't pray at all.

Renee: No?

Stephanie: I don't go to church. I don't believe in that stuff. I believe in the church of common sense.

Renee: That's funny. I love that you can make jokes.

Stephanie: I use humor to keep my sanity. I have a personal moral code instead of a set religion. My code certainly isn't based on fear and intimidation. Strange, now it feels like that's how my marriage was.

Renee: Did you used to belong to a religion? Pat, is this too much off topic?

Pat: No, not at all. Stephanie, do you want to talk about religion if it's part of your life?

Stephanie: Okay. Religion isn't a barrier to divorce for me, if that's what you mean. I used to have a religion I believed was pure, wholesome, loving, and nurturing. But behind the pulpit were some dark realities. I became disillusioned and left my church. I'm becoming disillusioned with my marriage too. Did the man I met and fell in love with even exist, or did I fall in love with an ideal he created until I was completely hooked, much like a cult process?

I know I loved the man I married and the partnership and family I thought we created. That ideal is hard for me to give up, especially because he could be so tender, affectionate, and make me feel like the most beautiful, appreciated, and loved person on the planet—when it suited him. I used to tell myself how lucky I was, and that all couples have challenges. That was a long time ago. Being a good person is my religion now. Karma dictates my choices, direction in life, and how I treat people. That is my religion.

Renee: Well, I have to admit my faith has been tested, but I still go to church. It helps me.

Pat: Everyone has to make a decision about faith, religion, and spirituality. This is a personal choice, and you will each decide in your own way.

To switch topics a bit, all three of you have "other women" to deal with. Renee and Debbie, your ex's cheated on you while you were married. Stephanie, your husband is already dating. You should all be angry and hurt by your husbands' betrayal, and also angry that another woman would disregard your marriage. Stephanie, you used the word *cougar*, which in this case means a woman who prowls after married men for one night stands or short relationships.

Debbie: How can our society function if we don't respect the institution of marriage?

Pat: That's an excellent question.

Renee: I remember something else. The babysitter who took care of my kids while I was at work told me that one day, she noticed my ex wasn't wearing his wedding band. She asked him why. Apparently, I had already left for work. He told her not wearing a wedding ring helped keep women from coming on to him, because they only want married men for the thrill of the conquest. She told me she couldn't believe he said that. She was his employee, so she kept it to herself at the time. Much later, she was disgusted when I told her the things he'd done.

Pat: Your husbands and these women are all betraying the institution of marriage. Chasing married men for the challenge is a sad reflection on our society. It's like these women are not part of the human tribe. They don't care about the wives, children, and families they may be destroying. It is said that loving the mother of his children is a father's most important role. All of your husbands betrayed their vows to you and their important roles as fathers.

Now I want you to think about something that may be hard to hear. It may be better that your husbands are dating or even marrying other women.

Debbie: Why? That sounds crazy.

Pat: Renee and Stephanie, your husbands are sociopaths and narcissists. Debbie, your husband is an alcoholic and a narcissist. We'll talk more about those diagnoses in a later session. These men can't survive without having a relationship for show, for cover, or whatever. They live to manipulate others. Most divorced men who abuse their wives remarry or at least start dating and even living with someone soon after the break up, if not before. You should know that whoever they're with is keeping them away from you. These other women are distracting him from you.

Stephanie: I think you're right. He stopped bothering me so much.

Debbie: It's not fair though. Why didn't my husband love me?

Pat: No, it isn't fair and it still hurts. But that's reality. If I can offer any comfort, your husbands will eventually abuse the other women in their lives, just as they abused you. None of them can stay on good behavior for long.

Renee: My husband emailed my daughter that he's getting married again. I feel nothing about it, except that whoever she is will eventually find out what a pile of dung he is. She either doesn't know his past, or she knows and is going to marry him anyway. I just don't care at all.

Debbie: Do you want me to find out who she is?

Renee: Absolutely not. She's non-existent to me, and I want him that way too. I hope they move to South America.

Pat: Wherever your ex ends up, Renee, you can work on building psychic distance from him. We've talked about that before in individual therapy, and we can revisit it.

Reader: I don't get how some women want to destroy other people's marriages. How can they sleep at night? And it must be awful to bump into your ex-husband with another woman. I would want my ex-husband to move far away or just have a heart attack and die. After all, he broke my heart.

Session Eight

I Wish He Would Die

Pat: How is everyone feeling today?

Debbie: I am so furious. I had a hearing with Cheater and his lawyer. They filed a motion that will keep me away from the restaurant, but he refuses to cooperate with our request for documents. He just filed with the court the same financial statements he filed last year—and the judge got mad at ME! I know he's hiding money, and I know his banker is helping him. He even turned our employees against me. Sometimes I fantasize Cheater will be run over by his own truck driven by his trashy girlfriend in the driveway of the new house he bought after our divorce became final. Oh, and I saw on his Facebook page that he plans to marry her next month. Unbelievable.

Renee: It would serve him right to be run over by his own truck. For me, I wish something biblical would end my ex's life—maybe a bolt of lightning. Or even better, he gets arrested and jailed for prostituting a woman and he dies of AIDS in jail. Then everyone would know what a hypocrite he is. I don't want to kill him. I just don't want to ever be near him again, and I do wish he was dead. I don't like having these thoughts, but I have them. Basically, I just want justice for exploding our family.

49

Stephanie: Hmmm. Justice sounds good. I don't wish my husband would die. He's my children's father. I just want him to stop drinking and become a different man.

Pat: It's actually natural and common to think "what if he died," or to wish him dead. I hear that kind of thinking a lot in my practice. Most women are surprised when I tell them thinking this way is typical. So recognize it's normal to think, "life would be so much better and easier if he just died," but don't take it any further than that. You want to stay clear of him as much as possible, and you don't want to do anything rash and foolish that would land you in jail. All of your kids need you to be the nurturing parent; so keep your head and think straight. Being a widow instead of a divorcee might seem easier, but you need freedom and dignity, not revenge.

Acknowledge your feelings and then pay attention to the next steps in the separation, divorce, and healing process. You've all learned—or you're now learning—that divorce doesn't change your husbands into nice guys. If anything, the process makes them less rational and more enraged. Each of your husbands thinks you're at fault for everything, but don't let this behavior take your focus off the goal. An amicable separation or divorce is great when it works, but that doesn't apply in your cases. Create good lives for yourselves. Instead of looking for revenge, look for the freedom to build a better life.

Reader: It's hard to hear about all these terrible men and how they harmed their wives. I hope each of these women can learn to have a happier life. Sometimes we women tend to blame ourselves for everything.

My Husband

I heard the word. I knew its meaning.

But I had never felt it.

I never felt anguish before you.

Fear and anger: Who knew those feelings could even be paired?

I knew their meanings,

but I never felt this fear and anger before you.

I thought opposites were just that, occupying separate tracks.

I never felt grief with relief before I met you.

Deep panic, waves of anxiety,

but I know I am safer now that it's through.

I've never hated anyone before,

and that's all that's left of you.

–Renee

Session Nine

I Feel So Stupid

Pat: How is everyone feeling tonight?

Debbie: Today I feel like I've messed up my entire life. I feel stupid.

Pat: Stupid? Why?

Debbie: I feel stupid because I married a lying, cheating thief. I didn't see the obvious signs.

Pat: Please help us understand what you mean.

Debbie: Like, Cheater told me soon after we bought the restaurant that I didn't need to go there at all. He told me I should focus on my job, which paid our bills for the first few years of our marriage, and then on the children. He worked a lot, and when he was home all he did was watch TV. I'm supposed to be the smart one in my family. I went to college. I had a career and was co-owner of our restaurant. I should've asked more questions and checked up on him and his drinking. I'm furious at him, but I'm angrier at myself.

Stephanie: I feel the same way. I don't know how I ended up with a mean drunk with no ambition. I have a degree in sociology.

Sharon: I graduated from college and worked in advertising before I got married. I didn't ever think married life would be this hard.

Renee: I've always thought of myself as an intelligent person, but I don't feel so smart now. I made excellent grades in school and earned a graduate degree in accounting, but I had no clue what the person closest to me was doing—or how long it was going on. His criminal, disgusting behavior lasted for years, and I had no idea. This whole thing has me wondering if I know anything about anything.

Debbie: We all have college degrees; we all had jobs, kids, and managed our households. Yet we totally botched our lives by marrying bad men. How could we be so stupid?

Stephanie: I don't like to think of myself as stupid, because that's what my husband calls me—a stupid b—. I'm not stupid, and I'm not a b—.

Pat: That's right, you're not stupid. In fact, you are all smart women, and most certainly not stupid. Banish that word from your minds. What all of you have in common are husbands who betrayed your trust. You trusted them to respect and care for you and your children. Instead, they went on drinking binges, chased other women, bought sex from prostitutes, and demeaned you. You were criticized, hit, shoved, and in Renee's case, given an STD. You didn't know any of that when you married them, though it's possible there were red flags. You loved and trusted your husbands, and that is normal. That's exactly what you were supposed to do. And remember each of these men said he loved you. Each man led you to believe there was love in your marriage, but what happened to you is not love. Also, every one of your husbands fooled a lot of people—not just you. Being fooled is different from being stupid. If anything, I believe your strong intellects and accomplishments made you think you could solve the big problems in your marriages. Next session we'll talk about why you chose these men.

Reader: So smart women can choose bad husbands. But why, and how, does that happen?

Session Ten:

Why Did I Choose Him?

The Charmer

Pat: Stephanie, why did you choose your husband? Tell us about dating him.

Stephanie: I met my husband at a bar. Funny to admit that now, when I realize he's an alcoholic. My cousin introduced us during my last year of college. My husband-to-be was already an apprentice electrician with a good job. He was cute and funny. My cousin told me later that he zeroed in on me as soon as I walked through the door, which made me feel special. He asked me out, I agreed, and the rest is history. Or tragedy.

Pat: Was drinking a problem then?

Stephanie: Local bars were the main place to socialize when I was in college. Lots of bars surround the campus, and most of them were hang outs where you could meet someone you knew almost any night of the week—especially Thursday through Sunday. He usually drank beer, and so did our friends. People smoked pot also. He told great stories and had an excellent sense of humor. Even after we married, when we went out it was almost always to a bar where we'd meet up with friends. That changed for me when I got pregnant. After my boys were born, I didn't go out much, but he still did—first on weekends and then more and more.

Pat: What about you, Debbie? Did your husband used to drink a lot?

Debbie: I met Cheater after school while I was working for a hotel chain. He's four years older than me and he was already managing a restaurant. I love good food, so right away we had that in common. He was interesting and seemed refined. He was also good looking, at least in my opinion, and I liked his family, especially his mother. She liked me too. Our dates were usually late at night after he closed the restaurant or on Mondays when the place was closed. He told me he'd always dreamed of owning his own restaurant, and I thought that was a wonderful ambition. Soon, I began to share his vision. He asked me to marry him, and I accepted. I worked hard to save money and we eventually bought our restaurant. Because it wasn't a sure thing, I kept my job with the hotel so we'd have a steady income.

Renee: I met my ex in graduate school, so we started off having something in common. Many of us would hang out together in the school cafeteria, at a particular bar downtown, or in the library. Being with him felt easy and safe. We might have a few beers, but drinking wasn't a problem. However, he smoked cigarettes and also smoked a lot of pot. I wasn't into smoking pot or drinking. Maybe I should have recognized this was a warning sign that we were different in our approach to drug use, but I thought he was fascinating. I liked that he played the piano. He tried to quit smoking cigarettes for me, and even though he couldn't quit, I was touched that he tried. We studied together and stayed together at night. This seemed romantic to me at the time. He made me goofy cards, wrote poetry for me, and sang to me when we were dating. I felt special. A few times during our marriage he'd surprise me, like making a big sign on the front of the house when we brought our first child home. And once he drew a red heart in the snow in our yard after a big storm.

Sharon: My husband can be sweet too, and his outgoing personality makes him the life of the party. In fact, I met him at a party in New York. He's smart—he has a master's degree in chemistry—and he works hard. He's been promoted many times at his company. He was attentive to me at first. We had a fancy wedding, and bought a house and furniture right away. I quit my job after my daughter was born. I thought I had it made. I had exactly the life I wanted. Then everything changed.

Pat: You are all accomplished women and were attracted to charming, even magnetic, men who had great potential. That is understandable. From what each of you shared about your husbands, we know they're expert manipulators.

Reader: All these couples seemed normal to me at the beginning of their relationships. Is that right? Did the men select these women for a reason?

Session Eleven

Why Did He Choose Me?

The Denier

Pat: What do you think your husbands saw in you?

Stephanie: I think my husband saw me as a drinking buddy, but I never drank as much as he did.

Pat: That's probably right. So what do you think happened?

Stephanie: Well, I grew up and I thought he'd grow up, too. After you become parents, you shouldn't go out drinking every night. Parents should be home, sober, and building a happy family life. I kept thinking he'd realize this, and I told him so. I told myself, "Maybe he can't relate to infants." Then it was, "Maybe he can't relate to toddlers." And that's how it went over the years. Now my boys are teenagers and my husband goes to some of their events, but not much else. And he's also drunk on many of these occasions; he yells at their games—shouts their names and tells them what to do in the game. It's awful pressure on the boys and embarrassing for me.

Pat: Stephanie, you keep waiting for your husband to grow up.

Stephanie: Yes. Part of me still thinks he'll see the light someday.

Pat: Maybe. Debbie, what about you?

Debbie: Well, my job with the hotel chain gave me a decent income. I thought Cheater loved me, but maybe he was just looking for someone to help get his dream restaurant and then stay out of his life. When I mentioned having children he was all for it, but he never was a doting father. We were both busy, but I thought we were building a life together. I told him he had to stop drinking and I thought he did. When I found out later he cheated on me, I thought I would die. Then I bought his apology and his promise never to do it again. I thought he loved me, but now I think he was playing me the whole time. Did he scope me out? Was I that gullible?

Pat: Sometimes men like your husbands consciously look for naïve, dependent women as victims. Even if this motivation is unconscious for them, they are definitely seeking women they can manipulate and control.

Renee, were you in denial about your ex?

Renee: For sure I was. When I look back, I used my smarts to make up excuses for my ex's behavior, and that blocked me from worse thoughts. I reasoned he was always busy and a bit eccentric. What a euphemism that was! He might have been a workaholic, but I had no idea he was leading a double life. Once I called him when he was at work to ask straight out if he was having an affair. I'd become suspicious because I barely saw him for a two week period. He shouted on the phone "I'm at work. I don't have time for an affair!" That's a long way from a statement of love, but somehow I felt reassured. He rarely told me he loved me, but his answer confirmed in my mind that he was working hard for the family, and I needed to be supportive. At the time, I was staying home and had my hands full with the kids.

I kept telling myself things would get better. Soon he'd manage to have more time for the family. Soon his family in New Hampshire would realize I was a good person and come to like me. Soon he'd be nicer to me. None of it ever happened. In the meantime, he criticized me more and more for everything, and if I challenged him directly he criticized me more. I didn't want that, so I held my tongue most of the time. That doesn't mean I was happy with the status quo, but I didn't feel he was walking all over me. Yet he was.

Pat: Do you see now that you were a perfect cover for his dark life of seediness and sex?

Renee: Yes, I absolutely see that now, and it makes me angry to realize how cleverly he turned my tolerance, hope, and patience into faults. He gave me just enough attention to string me along.

Pat: Also, sometimes we excuse and excuse a husband in order to protect ourselves from verbal and physical abuse. Your denial is a defense to avoid his constant insults.

Sharon, what started the relationship between you and your husband?

Sharon: From the time we met I was attracted to my husband and he seemed attracted to me. He sort of swept me off my feet by taking me to nice places and even traveling. He seemed like the marrying type, because he always talked about how much he wanted a family. He even told me he wanted three kids. I was happy to find a dependable man who would devote himself to me and our future children.

Now, he works a lot and acts like a drill sergeant about the smallest thing. Everything irritates him. He wants everything to be "just so," but raising children isn't like that. I feed the kids dinner, bathe them and put them to bed before he gets home. Then he and I usually have dinner and watch TV. He insists I sit right next to him on the couch. Going to bed has been awful lately; he tells me what to wear or not wear. Sex is getting rougher. Once when I said no, he threw me on the bed and raped me. He told me never to say no to him again. If I try to stand up for the kids just being kids, he gets extremely angry. Once he pushed me out of the house and locked the doors, because he said I let the kids go wild. He finally let me back in, saying he did it to teach me a lesson. So, I make sure the kids have their rambunctious time when he isn't around. I tell them "Daddy's tired, so don't be noisy." This doesn't always work. He will pick up whichever kid is irritating him and literally toss that child into a bedroom and slam the door.

Pat: I wasn't sure you were going to share the rape incident with the group. I'm glad you had the courage to talk about it, Sharon.

Debbie: Is that rape, or is it domestic abuse?

Pat: Both. In abusive relationships, marital rape is seen fairly often. Women in abusive marriages often second guess marital rape by convincing themselves it was just rough sex. But, if you say *no* and your spouse continues, it's marital rape.

The coping mechanism of denial works for a while, until it doesn't work anymore. His need to control you and the kids is increasing. Pushing you out of the house and throwing you across the garage is a sign of more violence to come.

Sharon: Or maybe his work is becoming too high pressure for him.

Pat: Sharon, your husband and all of these men found women who give them wide latitude to behave badly. No level of pressure at work justifies your husband's abusive behavior to you and the children.

Reader: This is awful! But how can we know which men to avoid? These guys don't walk around with danger signs on their chests!

Session Twelve

Ignoring the Red Flags

Pat: Each of you realized at some point that you were living with someone wildly different from the person you thought you married. In hindsight, can you see any red flags you missed?

Stephanie: My husband comes from a family of drinkers. I did not. For them, every family gathering seemed to be a race to get sauced and have a good time. Even his mother drank a lot. They called her Mummy Rummy. His sarcastic and domineering father was the center of all activity. They often talked about politics and entertainers with mocking insults and negative comments. My family life was totally different. We had normal conversations at dinner, usually about school stuff and our activities. We didn't shout at each other or swear, and we only drank wine on special occasions. Being young when we met, I had no idea his family was dysfunctional, but I knew they were different.

Renee: I can't think of any red flags in my case—except my ex once slept with another student after we started dating, but we'd only been dating a few months. I broke up with him over that and told him to get lost. Then he wrote me a letter and even sang a love song under my window asking for forgiveness. When we talked, he said he'd never do that again. I believed him, and we started dating again. Was that a red flag? If anything, I thought he got the message that I wouldn't accept such behavior. About a year later, I moved in with him. We moved to the same city together after grad school, and then we got engaged. As far as I knew, he was always faithful until he told me a few years ago I should go to a doctor to be checked for gonorrhea.

Pat: Was he critical of you before marriage?

Renee: When we first started dating, he asked me, "Why do you wear shoes like that?" I owned one pair of worn sneakers and a pair of plain black flats that were out of fashion. I told him in no uncertain terms that I didn't have a lot of money and I had to save the money I earned waitressing for tuition, books, rent, and food. He had all that given to him by his parents. He shut up about my clothes after that, but the criticism resumed after we married.

Also, he once bragged to me that he dated a girl who won a beauty contest. I said, "Big deal!" and told him he should leave if looks were that important to him. He didn't bring it up again. I thought I knew him and we'd worked everything out because we dated for three years before marrying. His family was never friendly to me, but we weren't going to live in the same state, so I didn't worry about them. Biting comments happened often in that family. Dinner at his house included sarcasm and criticism of other people. They seemed to thrive on gossip and unkindness.

Stephanie: What about when you got engaged?

Renee: We announced our engagement at dinner at their place in New Hampshire. His parents seemed resigned to it, and asked when we planned the ceremony. Then the conversation went to having children, and his mom started talking about abortions. Totally inappropriate. This wasn't a dinner filled with smiles and joy. We planned for our wedding in a few months, though we were already living together. I remember an especially painful incident leading up to the wedding. His mother didn't like my wedding dress, which was my mom's wedding dress. When I tried it on for her I was all happy and giggly—and then she told me a seamstress could make it over. That was her only comment. I told her I planned to wear it just as it was. Neither of my in-laws ever said they were happy I'd be joining their family. Ever. I can't recall a single kind word, even at the wedding. I just put these negatives in the back of my mind and focused on starting a life with my husband in a new state.

Pat: Did you talk to your husband about this?

Renee: Yes, of course. He told me I was marrying him, not his parents, so I should relax. He never stood up to his parents.

Pat: It's certainly a problem when your husband's family doesn't support your marriage. The red flags become clearer in hindsight. What about you, Debbie?

Debbie: I don't recall any red flags. He drank some when we dated, but not to excess. I guess I really didn't know how much he was drinking in the restaurant business. He seemed to come from a good, close family, although I think he was spoiled by his doting mother. He has a couple of sisters and was the only boy, so Mama and the sisters babied him. He didn't have a father figure, because his dad died when he was four years old. Hmmm... as I talk I begin to see the red flags I never noticed. I guess he was used to using women to get what he wanted. Interesting.

Pat: Sometimes we don't hear any blaring alarms, or the signs are well hidden. Did you see any red flags, Sharon?

Sharon: My husband was never physically abusive before we married, and he wasn't critical of me, my clothes, or how I acted. He used to comment on how lucky he felt being engaged to me. He had an air of entitlement about him, and he was used to getting things his way. He exuded confidence and competence, which I found attractive. As I said, he was the life of every party and loved being the center of attention. He had strong opinions about everything and often commented on what other people were wearing and doing. Quite frankly, I figured it was better to be with someone who had strong opinions than a wishy washy person. I didn't realize his opinions about everything were a red flag for narcissism. I didn't even know what narcissism was until Pat told me about it.

I also look back on a conversation I had with his sister after my husband and I became engaged. She took me to lunch and I thought it was a "get to know you better" lunch. But instead of chit chat, she told me her brother had a bad temper and she gave me some examples of him throwing stuff and hitting people when they were younger. I told her I hadn't seen any of that, and I felt her brother had matured into a composed businessman.

Pat: She was trying to warn you.

Sharon: Yes, I see that now. I also remember how nervous my husband was when he asked me what his sister and I talked about at lunch. I didn't tell him, of course. His sister made me promise I wouldn't tell him anything. Now I see that she was still afraid of him.

Reader: I hope I would see some of those red flags, but I think I would have missed some, too. After all, you're in love, right? But now I see how important it is to get to know a man and his extended family before marriage.

Session Thirteen

I Can Fix Him. He Will Change.

Pat: Debbie and Renee, you stayed married even after big problems occurred in your marriages. Why? Did you try to fix your husbands?

Debbie: Yes. I told Cheater he had to stop drinking, and he said he would. I told him NEVER to cheat on me again, and he said he wouldn't. I thought he saw the error of his ways and realized he'd lose me if he cheated again. I planned nice evenings for us, hoping he'd fall in love with me again. I was wrong to believe he'd change for me and the kids. He lied to me, cheated on me, and stole from the business to pay for his party life.

Pat: Your ex is an alcoholic. Drinking became the thing he cared most about. What about you, Renee?

Renee: Looking back, I put up with a lot of mean and neglectful behavior, but I just kept plugging away, thinking he'd change if I didn't complain too much. When I pointed things out to him, he'd tell me I was too sensitive. I knew he could be nice when he wanted to, but being nice was apparently not his norm. We went to a marriage counselor after our fourth child was born, and the counselor sent my ex to a psychiatrist. That was a good idea, because the psychiatrist diagnosed bi-polar disorder and ADD. He was given medications, and as far as I knew, he took his meds. I thought the medicines would fix him. I convinced myself he was better. We even decided to renew our marriage vows when our fourth child was baptized. That's how hopeful I was. Can you imagine? To be honest, the bad times were less frequent, but not because he was better. He just spent even more time at work. Or so I thought.

Pat: Unfortunately, Renee, no pill can correct character flaws, and few therapeutic techniques can treat personality problems like narcissistic disorder or sociopathic disorder.

Stephanie: My husband has been drinking steadily and smoking pot more, and he just gets meaner. My house could be perfect, and he'd still find something to yell about. I've asked him many times to stop drinking, go to AA, and to stop shouting at me and the kids. He refuses. At least the house is quiet since he moved out.

Sharon: If I suggested to my husband that he has a problem, he'd go crazy on me.

Pat: AA has helped many people and we can talk about that later. Stephanie, I'm pretty sure your husband has more going on than alcoholism. And Sharon, your husband has some very deep problems. You can't make perfect homes for your husbands, and even if you could, that won't be enough for them.

Listen, you are smart women who are used to setting and achieving your goals with hard work. You got A's in school and succeeded at work. So it's understandable that you thought you could fix your husbands' bad behavior through creativity, patience, and persistence.

Renee: I didn't want to admit failure.

Debbie: Me neither.

Pat: You are not failures. Look, each one of your husbands has shown that they don't share your values and don't have the same family priorities as you do. You don't have much chance of changing another person's basic values. You can talk until you're blue in the face, and it won't help .For your own wellbeing, all of you need to understand that you can never change another person; you can only change how you respond to that person. People only change when they are motivated to change, and it doesn't seem any of your husbands think they have problems and need to change. Please stop banging your heads against brick walls. You will be the only one who gets banged up and bloody.

Reader: So these guys were all jerks. If you've married a jerk and have kids, should you divorce right away or hang in there for the kids?

Session Fourteen

Why Did I Stay with Him?

Keeping the Family Together

Pat: You all have children. Let's share with each other how having children affected your decisions. Renee?

Renee: My mindset was to keep on trying to improve my marriage especially for the sake of my children, but my fall back strategy was to keep as low a profile as possible. I really thought staying at home fulltime to care for our children after my fourth was born would make life more manageable for him. He was also on meds and supposedly working through his problems with a therapist. I wanted him to somehow transform into a wonderful family man. My two oldest kids did grow up and my daughter moved to another city. My second oldest was in his last month of college when the gonorrhea bomb blew up. His graduation day was awful for me. My other son was in college too and away at the time. My sons moved out as soon as they could. I'm now at home with my daughter, even though she's an adult.

Pat: What if your kids were still little when you filed for divorce?

71

Renee: Everything would have been worse. I would have fought for full custody and no visitations for my pervert husband who had prostituted hundreds of women and gave me gonorrhea. Now, all of our children are adults and have nothing to do with him. Thank goodness. The divorce was about dividing assets and nothing more.

Stephanie: My two boys are teenagers now and one of them is struggling in community college. When they were young, it would have been hard to take care of everything as single parent. At least my husband would drive my kids to practice and games and the mall. Also, I always thought boys needed a father. Now I wonder if that was a huge mistake.

Pat: Why?

Stephanie: My boys have seen their father drunk and mean and calling their mother a stupid b----. What a bad role model. Now my sons yell at me all the time and at each other. They also drink at parties and friends' houses. I'm sure of that, even though neither of them is old enough to drink. The judge who issued the restraining order mandated anger management classes and AA for my husband. He had to go to the anger classes, but I think he only went to AA meetings once or twice. Now the restraining order lifted and he hasn't changed at all. I guess if I decided to divorce my husband when my sons were young, they might be more respectful to me. At this point I think it's too late to change this.

Debbie: Cheater wasn't around much, so looking back I functioned as a single parent to our kids. But for a long time I focused on keeping the family intact. My kids are the most important thing to me. They were always in the back of my mind when I tried so hard to make our marriage work after he promised never to cheat on me again.

Pat: One benefit of waiting and enduring as long as you did, Renee and Debbie, was that your divorces didn't include a custody battle. This protected your children from being cared for by fathers who are alcoholics or narcissistic sociopaths addicted to sex and porn. Stephanie, your sons are old enough now to make their own decisions about where they'll live if you get a divorce.

Debbie: Yeah, but there can still be problems having older kids. For example, I was supposed to get child support until my kids graduated from college, and my daughter did attend college. Cheater was immediately in arrears for it, but he lied and told the judge he was broke because I took money from the business. That's a complete fabrication.

Pat: Divorce ends a marriage, but it doesn't transform your ex into a good father. Sharon, your children are still little. What do you think about this topic?

Sharon: I think that if we didn't have kids, I'd have filed for divorce long ago. Now I'm afraid he'll fight tooth and nail for joint custody. Then my kids would be with him for periods of time when I can't keep them safe and buffer them from his criticism. I would also need child support and alimony to live, and he would micro-manage every penny. So I don't see any good choices. For my kids, I'll do anything, including staying married to a controlling man.

Debbie: If you ever don't feel safe, you can come to my house.

Sharon: Thank you. Fortunately, I have a good friend who lives nearby.

Pat: Many women wait until their kids are older before they file for divorce, but you should never tolerate physical or emotional violence for the sake of your children. Your children are victims too, directly or indirectly. And as Stephanie said, they will have a bad role model for a father, and they see their mothers as tolerating it. Not much gets by your kids, though you may not want to think so.

Reader: What if the husband has a change of heart? Is there ever hope for the relationship?

Session Fifteen

I Feel Sorry For Him.

Is Reconciliation an Option?

Pat: Sharon is wondering if reconciliation is ever possible.

Sharon: Well, if my husband would ever agree to go to therapy like Renee's husband, maybe he would get better.

Renee: That's what I hoped and prayed for, but my ex still lived his secret life of prostitutes and porn and he lied to me every single day. For all I know, he was lying to his therapist.

Pat: Didn't you try to do even more, like helping him get informed on topics?

Renee: Yeah, like an idiot, I did. I gave him articles about the exploitation of women and how most prostituted women were victims of abuse or neglect when they were growing up. I wanted him to realize he was taking advantage of desperate women. I found out where sex addiction groups were meeting and told him to go get help. I rationalized that I took vows to care for him in sickness and in health, and maybe he was sick. I suggested he check into a mental health hospital for a week or two and tell work he was on vacation. He thought I was being ridiculous.

Later, after my brother died, he told me he saw the light and wanted to recommit to our marriage. I was in such an emotional state, I agreed to let him come home, but it lasted about a week. He soon became mean and tyrannical and he criticized me about the funeral service and my questions to the lawyer about my brother's probate estate. He criticized everything. I can't believe I even considered reconciliation for one minute. How could I be so dumb?

Pat: What happened? And you're not dumb!

Renee: He came back at me with how all men think about sex all the time, porn is normal, men are never monogamous, and I'm the one with the problem. His favorite comment to me was, "What's your problem?" He also told me the working girls he went to thought he was a good customer because he didn't beat them. He actually told me he was helping these women by letting them earn money. He makes me sick.

Pat: His statements disgust me, too. Debbie, what about you? Was reconciliation ever a possibility?

Debbie: Yes, after he promised me he'd never be unfaithful again, I was willing to stay in the marriage and try hard to make it work. But he didn't try at all. I think he was buying time so he wouldn't have to split our assets in a divorce. He never truly acted like he cared about me or the kids. He is a cheater and I hate him.

Pat: Stephanie, if your husband stayed in AA, do you think you would reconcile with him?

Stephanie: I think so, yes, but not if he choked me again.

Sharon: If my husband could be transformed into a good man, I'd be so happy. Maybe if he went to therapy, but Renee says that even with medicine and therapy, her husband didn't change.

Pat: Sociopaths and narcissists like your husbands do not have treatable conditions such as an anxiety problem, bipolar disorder, or depression.

Sharon: Are sociopaths and narcissists common?

Pat: Unfortunately, yes, and your husbands mostly fit into these categories.

Reader: All these women wanted to save their marriages, so they tried and tried again, to no avail it seems.

Who Are These Men?

Session Sixteen

The Sex Addict/Porn Addict

Pat: We've been talking about how you feel foolish for selecting husbands who turned out to be . . .to be . . .

Debbie: Bums.

Pat: Okay, bums. Let's focus on the bums for a while. Renee told me that learning about her husband's problems from a clinical perspective helped her realize he was dysfunctional, although she enabled him. All your husbands have deep seated problems. That's why I think you ladies will benefit from sharing your stories with each other. So let's start with Renee. Tell us about the sex stuff.

Renee: Well, you all know my ex gave me gonorrhea. I think I also told you he said it was a mistake when he got drunk and bought a prostitute, and it only happened one time. A couple of weeks later, when I demanded he tell me everything, he vomited out his whole disgusting, slimy life. He estimated 650 times with prostitutes and other women he knew. What kind of number is that? Does he have a tally board at work? I asked him when it all started, and he said after the birth of our first child when he had sex with a summer office helper. If I'd known he was cheating on me then, I could've left him while I still had a career.

Pat: So he knew exactly when it began, right?

Renee: Yes. He said, "It started a long time ago," like he was telling me a bedtime story. One of the guys at work got him into phone sex. He said he first did it as a joke, and then he started doing it all the time. He watched porn every day on his office computer masturbating right there in his office chair. How gross. I assume this was after hours when he didn't come home because—as he told me and the kids—he had so much work to do. Yeah, right. He said he couldn't recall the date when he first prostituted a woman, but he remembers how nervous he felt. Well, he obviously got over the nerves and continued the act 650 times. He described it all, and seemed proud of how clever he was not to get caught.

Besides reeling with shock and disgust, I could hardly believe how this could happen and develop as it did. I had the proof though: my gonorrhea. And all this went on while he was in therapy for more than twelve years with a psychologist, and also taking meds from a therapist. I asked him if his doctors knew about the prostitutes and having sex with a teenager, and he said no. He didn't tell them until after he got gonorrhea and gave it to me. He told me he informed his doctors then, but I have no clue whether he did or not. He lies to everybody.

Pat: You did research on sex addiction?

Renee: Yes. I went online for information and then scoured the psychology section of the local bookstore. We also talked a lot about sex addiction in my sessions with you, Pat. At first I had no clue sexual addiction was possible.

Pat: Sex addiction is unfortunately becoming more common in our society with the prevalence of pornography on the internet. You can reach pornography sites with a single click of the mouse. It's easy and free—at first. The same compulsive behavior that characterizes other addictions is typical of sex addiction. The National Council on Sexual Addiction and Compulsivity defines sexual addiction as "engaging in persistent and escalating patterns of sexual behavior acted out despite increasing negative consequences to self and others."

In other words, a sex addict will continue engaging in certain sexual behaviors despite facing potential health risks, financial problems, shattered relationships, and even arrest. People addicted to sex get a sense of euphoria that seems greater than most people experience, but intimacy is always missing. For sexual addicts, sex isn't about intimacy. Addicts use sex to seek pleasure, avoid unpleasant feelings, or respond to outside stress. This is similar to how an alcoholic uses alcohol.

Sexual offenders who act out their addiction are not using sex for physical gratification, but rather out of a disturbed need for power, dominance, control, revenge, or even a perverted expression of anger. Data from recent studies shows the brain changes and brain rewards associated with sexual behavior may help explain the powerful compulsion motivating sexual addicts and offenders. *The Porn Trap* by Wendy and Larry Maltz is an excellent book for understanding sexual addiction.

Attending Al Anon meetings is one of the best things you can do to get a grip on how the addiction affects you. I recommend Al Anon if you can't find a specific support group for family members of sex addicts. As with alcoholic co-dependent behavior, if you're enabling a sex addict, it's important for you to understand his behavior and your reactions.

Renee: Right. You told me what to do and I found an Al Anon group meeting near my house. I didn't know what to expect. My nerves were on edge as we went around the room that first night, but before I introduced myself, a couple of people talked about being there because a child in the family was addicted to drugs. So I quickly realized not everyone there had alcoholism in their families. I was the only one who lived with a sex addict, and after the meeting a woman came up to me and said some people in the group might be uncomfortable because of the sex addiction stuff I mentioned, so she recommended I leave out the sex part and just say my husband is an addict. How about that? I had a husband with an addiction so awful it made people squirm at an Al Anon meeting! But I took her advice. I went to meetings almost every week for more than a year, and I read the brochures and the little books of daily advice. Some of the stuff seemed spot on, but other things were difficult to accept.

Debbie: Like what?

Renee: I was invested with my wrong thinking, like "I can fix him," and "I must be some crappy person if my husband has done all this to me." Al Anon and the 12 steps are geared to detaching and recognizing that the addict's behavior is on him. All a family member can do is work to change her own life. Also, we can't change the past, only the future. Stuff like that. I put one of Al Anon's sayings on my fridge: *Don't take it personally*. Still, I had trouble with that idea.

Pat: Why?

Renee: I told myself, "When someone's criticizing me and calling me names, how can that not be personal? No one else is in the room." But now I know the Al Anon people are right. I think you might get a lot out of Al Anon, Stephanie.

Pat: How did phone sex and computer sex factor into the divorce proceedings?

Renee: My lawyer obtained a record of my husband's calls and credit card bills, which proved a lot. If necessary, she was prepared to get his computer hard drive.

Pat: Renee, you now understand that the abuse and disrespect your husband showed you are his problems, and they don't reflect on who you are.

Renee: Would you tell us the symptoms of sexual addiction?

Pat: When someone is addicted to sex, he or she is constantly thinking of sex to the detriment of other activities; continually engaging in excessive sexual practices; spending considerable time in activities related to sex, such as cruising for partners or spending hours online visiting porn web sites; continually engaging in the sexual behavior despite negative consequences, such as broken relationships or potential health risks; escalating the scope or frequency of sexual activity to achieve the desired effect, such as more frequent visits to prostitutes or more sex partners;

and feeling irritable when unable to engage in the desired behaviors. This addiction is especially difficult to treat, and few support groups exist just for sex addiction.

Debbie: How did your husband react when you told him going to prostitutes was exploitation?

Renee: Oh, he said he was just a good customer. When I said he objectifies women, he said he loves women and that sex is everywhere. "What's your problem?" he asked me. He blamed me for everything and said he had to go out and carouse because his life was crap.

Pat: Blaming others is a common part of most addictions. Renee, as you now realize, your ex showed misogyny, not love and respect for women. And remember, you're a woman, so he used you, too.

Stephanie: What's misogyny?

Pat: Basically, it is hatred for all women and a desire to use and abuse them. If you look up the word in the dictionary it derives from Greek misein (to hate) and gyne (woman). It is not love by a long shot. Unfortunately, in our society misogyny often masquerades as sexual freedom. Using women for sex and demeaning women for sexual gratification are forms of misogyny. Prostituting women is not done to show love; rather it is to demean women and show power and control over them. Men who go to prostitutes are the opposite of women lovers; they are women haters.

Renee: It seems to me his actions of degrading women through prostitution and porn were also aimed at me.

Debbie: What do you mean?

Renee: Well, he knows I've always been interested in equal rights, equal opportunity, and equal pay for women. So, I'm a feminist. For him to develop a secret life degrading and exploiting women is a cruel personal attack on me and my values, not to mention the harm he caused other women.

Pat: Your ex has a long list of issues along with the sex and porn addictions. I don't doubt his behavior that developed into addictions was also narcissistic and sociopathic. Many of the conditions I see in your husbands' behaviors co-exist with other conditions. Because alcohol addiction often coincides with sexual addiction, let's focus on alcoholism next session and talk about the other issues later.

     Reader: I had no idea different addictions had so many similarities. I see in the news that sexual and porn addiction are becoming more common, but I hadn't thought about what they can do to families.

Session Seventeen

The Alcoholic Abuser

Pat: Welcome to the session, everyone. At our last meeting Renee shared that her husband was addicted to porn and sex. Stephanie and Debbie's husbands have problems with alcohol. Is it okay to continue discussing addictions tonight, with a focus on alcoholism?

Stephanie: Yes, it's fine. I need all the help I can get!

Pat: And that's why we're here—to help each other.

Stephanie: I need a "do over" for my life. Can anybody here help with that?

Debbie: I know exactly what you mean, Stephanie. Everywhere I turned there was another mess with me in the middle.

Renee: I also remember feeling I was losing control, like a spinning top. Then I found out that having control is only fiction, and I need to be okay with that.

Pat: You're right. Each of you kept trying to fix things as though you had the ability to change and control your husbands' behavior. But you don't. Stephanie, tell us again how drinking affected your life.

Stephanie: I met my husband in a bar, and most of our dates were at a bar or going to a bar after a movie. He drinks mostly beer. I drink wine and some beer, and sometimes there was hard liquor—like Margarita parties. Stuff like that. I pretty much stopped drinking when I got pregnant and had babies to look after, but he kept on chugging.

Pat: What about now?

Stephanie: He stops at that same bar almost every day on his way home from work, and he drinks a lot on weekends. He used to fall asleep at home in his chair watching TV. I guess he really passed out, right? He started forgetting to do things—like pick up the boys at a game. And, he yelled and swore at me all the time like I caused all this.

Pat: Could he stop drinking?

Stephanie: He used to say he could stop drinking whenever he wanted, but he didn't want to. Then he'd add, "So shut up, b - - - -."

Debbie: That is so familiar. Cheater didn't call me that name, but he always said he could stop drinking any time he wanted. I told him if he didn't stop drinking I'd leave with the kids –and they were still young. I think he did stop drinking, at least for a while.

Pat: Did he attend Alcoholics Anonymous? A lot of groups meet around here.

Debbie: No. He would tell me when I asked, that he hadn't had a drink in two weeks, or three months, or whatever. But now I realize Cheater is still an alcoholic. He could be mean and do destructive things whether he was drinking or not. I'm pretty sure he's drinking again. I see his party photos on Facebook and I spotted him and his girlfriend coming out of a liquor store.

Stephanie: Well, my husband won't go to AA, and he blames me for the breakup of our family and making everyone poor.

Pat: It's important to realize that alcoholics who won't admit they have a problem with alcohol are not going to change. They will continue blaming everyone else for their problems, rather than turning the mirror towards themselves. So, don't listen to an actively drinking alcoholic. They are almost always lying, and they definitely will blame you rather than accepting responsibility for their problems. Only the alcoholic can decide to change the course of his or her life. Debbie's husband did stop drinking for a while to keep the family together, but Stephanie, your husband is still drinking—right?

Stephanie: Oh, he is most certainly still drinking, and I wouldn't be surprised to learn he's also smoking pot. As far as I can tell, since he moved out he's at his bar every minute he isn't at work.

Pat: Right, and the recovery for Debbie's husband wasn't complete because he didn't get the additional support he needed from therapy, AA, or even a church. He is definitely not sober if he stooped so low as to take his children's bank accounts. Debbie, what's happening with the restaurant?

Debbie: The restaurant is in deep trouble. I don't do the books anymore, so I don't know the specifics, but I hear from our suppliers that Cheater owes a lot of money. You can't do business like that. The restaurant is barely functioning.

Pat: Alcoholics can change, and there are many success stories. But it looks like your husband, Stephanie, is not on that path. And whether Debbie's husband is drinking or not, he's still being self-destructive by buying a house with a new woman and her child while his business is spiraling downward. Alcoholism is a chronic and progressive disease that includes problems controlling your drinking, being preoccupied with alcohol, continuing to use alcohol even when it causes problems, having to drink more to get the same effects, or having physical withdrawal symptoms when you rapidly decrease or stop drinking.

Some alcoholics need to drink three or more alcoholic drinks daily, while others binge drink. A male binge drinker will drink more than five drinks in a row, and on another day may not drink at all.

Denying a problem with alcohol is usually part of alcoholism. Most alcoholics won't admit they have a problem until they have a bottoming out experience. This could be a DUI charge, losing a job due to drinking, or losing the family. For some alcoholics a bottoming-out that leads to recovery never occurs.

Stephanie: My husband denies he has a drinking problem and blames me for his need to drink. After he choked and hit me and I filed for a restraining order, I thought that would be a wake-up call for him to stop drinking. Apparently, the possibility of ending our marriage didn't make him hit bottom. I just don't matter to him. He hangs out with his brother and his buddies at the bar. I want to get him sober, but I haven't figured out how.

Pat: He has to want to change. It's you I'm concerned about now.

Stephanie: Well, if I come to you for therapy and have this support group, why do I need Al Anon? I don't have the time.

Renee: I know what you mean. I didn't have time either. I really don't know how I managed to go, but I just did. And it helped me a lot, so it may help you. My ex had a psychologist and a psychiatrist, and he still was leading a secret criminal life. Going to Al Anon gave me a lot to think about with my husband's sexual addiction, and then I'd talk to Pat about issues that came up for me at meetings. So therapy and Al-Anon both helped me, but this has been a long journey. I still have issues, but at least I don't feel like a spinning top.

Pat: Stephanie, please think about going to Al Anon, and your sons should go to Al A-Teen. Debbie, you too might benefit from it, even though you're divorced. Alcoholism leaves a long shadow on people around the drinker.

Renee: You're right. One of the women at my meeting was trying to deal with emotions about her alcoholic father even though he died years ago. That really surprised me.

Pat: I have one more thing to mention to those of you with alcoholic husbands or exes. I hate adding to your worries, but I think it's important for you to know there's strong evidence for a genetic link to alcoholism. You've seen alcoholics in your ex's families, and you should be mindful of your children. They may carry the gene, plus they grew up watching and learning drinking behavior from their fathers. Be especially vigilant as your sons and daughters go through adolescence. Forewarned is forearmed, as the saying goes.

Reader: Alcoholics cause their families a lot of pain. And it's scary to think their children could end up with the same problems. Are all these marriages bad because of addiction, or do they have other problems?

Session Eighteen

The Narcissistic Personality

Pat: During the last two sessions we focused on different types of addiction. We talked about sex addiction, addiction to pornography, and alcoholism. You're also dealing with husbands or ex husbands who have narcissistic personality disorder—or even worse, sociopathic personality disorder. Tonight, I'm going to describe the narcissistic personality. First, let me explain that personality disorders are a unique type of mental illness that often shows up in childhood or during the teenage years. These people have deep seated behavior patterns that touch almost every aspect of their lives—and the lives of people around them. You might say they play with different rules than the rest of us because they have no true feelings for others. And what is really interesting is that people with personality disorders don't realize their behavior and thought patterns are "off." They can't see any problems with their own thoughts and behavior, so they often blame their issues on others.

People with narcissistic personality disorder have an inflated sense of their own importance, a deep need for admiration, and a lack of empathy for others. Behind this mask of ultra-confidence lies a fragile self-esteem that's vulnerable to the slightest criticism. Living with a narcissistic person is difficult because they get angry and impatient when they don't receive special treatment. Narcissists come across as conceited, boastful, and pretentious. They tend to monopolize conversations and look down on others as inferior to them. Narcissists have trouble handling anything that may be perceived as criticism; they react with rage and contempt and try to belittle the other person to make themselves feel superior.

Renee: One of the things I talked to Pat about was how fragile my ex's ego seemed to be. If I made a comment about anything, he would quickly react with a put down of me. If we went to a movie, he'd ask me what I thought about it. If I liked it, he'd say, "Anyone could tell the cinematography was poor." If I said I didn't like the movie, he'd say "That was the best movie I've ever seen. What's wrong with you?"

This applied to dinners at restaurants, visits to families, a work of art, a book, TV shows, clothes—you name it. He'd ask me to comment first and then he'd say the opposite. He used Latin phrases or talk on and on about his travels, and then put me down if I asked what something meant. He'd say I didn't know anything because I grew up in a working class family and didn't go to private schools. If I cried, he'd say I was acting. My emotions would annoy him so much he'd leave the house.

Also, this may seem minor, but it sticks in my memory. Once when his aunt was at our house, she remarked that my flower garden was beautiful. The three of us were looking out the back window. He was standing next to me, and he wheeled around suddenly and stormed off. I think he couldn't stand to hear anyone else get a compliment, especially me.

Pat: I agree. What about his behavior when your brother died?

Renee: The latest examples of my ex's narcissistic behavior were around my brother's memorial service. My brother died suddenly in a truck accident at his job. He was only 50 years old.

Pat: What happened at the service?

Renee: My family and I decided to have the memorial service at a high school in my brother's hometown, because he was a volunteer soccer and golf coach at the school. My brother also volunteered at school events, like the annual food drive at Thanksgiving, car washes, stuff like that, and he always went to the graduation ceremonies. The school principal said he was always a great role model for the students. My brother was an all-around good guy. So one Saturday a few weeks after he died, we had a memorial service in the school auditorium. I gave a eulogy for the family—and others spoke too. The student choir sang. It was a beautiful celebration of my brother's life. Afterward, we had a reception in the cafeteria. I hired a caterer; the food was all spread out on tables with table cloths and flowers. We had photos of my brother with his teams and with our family. It was a beautiful day for all of us—except my husband. Instead of supporting me, he couldn't resist making snarky comments.

He said the fern I brought from home looked stupid and the scarf I wore with my dress looked pretentious. He also criticized me for not having enough drinks for the guests, and he was horrible the next day, too. He said he was tired of fetching things for me and my family. I had no idea what he was talking about, because everyone pitched in to make the memorial service beautiful. For crying out loud, I had just buried my brother!

Pat: Your husband's narcissism caused him to feel slighted by any attention given to you. He can't tolerate seeing you get compliments. Only his opinions matter and no rules apply to him—including fidelity in a marriage.

Renee: What about therapy for him?

Pat: Very few narcissists will admit they have a problem and therefore they won't use psychotherapy to try and work on personal relationships. They're also known to fake it during therapy, so most therapists won't attempt to treat these disorders. People like your husband are such good actors, and so entrenched, that even a therapist can't tell what's behind the façade. It takes years of commitment in therapy to make a dent in a personality disorder. Your husband may have gone to therapy for ADD and bi-polar disorder, but was silent about his life with porn and women he prostituted.

Renee: Was prostituting women part of his narcissism?

Pat: Yes. It has to do with control of others, in this case, women, and with self-gratification. You told us about the research you did about the addiction, poverty, abuse, and neglect in the lives of most women who end up as prostitutes. You told your husband how he exploited their misery, but he couldn't care less about them. It's all about him. And the risks involved with buying prostitutes or even having an affair just add to the thrill.

Renee: My husband actually told me he likes to be naughty. That was his word. Can you imagine a 55 year old accountant saying he likes to be naughty?

Debbie: Your husband is a creep.

Renee: Yup.

Stephanie: My husband also is a creep. He tells our boys to come to me for anything they need, because he's supposedly broke. Yet he goes to his bar every night, and his father still pays him a salary. He talks loud, tells gross jokes, and informs everyone he sees that he's suffering by having to live with his brother because his crazy wife threw him out. He tells lies to his family and our sons. He loves to wallow in their sympathy.

Pat: I agree. He wants attention for his woes and self-gratification with his drinking, smoking pot, and now dating. He believes none of his problems are caused by him and he wants the world to know it, because he's on stage all the time. That's why he needs to go to a bar after work— to find an audience.

Stephanie: You just reminded me of another show-off thing. My husband's family belongs to a club. Every Christmas, Thanksgiving, and Easter, the whole family goes to brunch in the club dining room. These meals are mandatory. Everything is picture perfect, including the clothes and food. They always take a group photo with his parents seated in the middle. Of course we all smile and look happy, no matter what we're really feeling. As far as I can make sense of it, this is all to show off for the other club members so his parents can pretend they have this great family.

Debbie: Why is it pretend? What do you mean?

Stephanie: Because some of the family members hate each other, my husband and his brother are usually drinking too much and getting obnoxious, and the grandchildren are basically ignored by my in-laws. Nothing is real about these brunches. The only thing my in-laws care about is having everyone there and all the males wearing jackets and ties. My boys know they shouldn't talk much except to say please and thank you. The conversations are superficial. No one seems to care if my husband is an alcoholic and abuses me. There's other stuff going on with his brothers and sister too. No one asks if I'm okay.

Pat: The sad thing is, they probably don't care about you. It's a command performance to make his family look good.

Reader: Wow, these narcissistic husbands are selfish and cruel. How does this differ from a sociopath?

Session Nineteen

The Sociopathic Personality

Pat: We spoke about narcissism last week, but another personality disorder is even more frightening and harmful. The name of this diagnosis has changed from psychopathic, to sociopathic, to antisocial personality disorder. I prefer to use the term sociopathic personality disorder, because I think antisocial personality disorder soft pedals these creepy people, and psychopath is used too loosely in the media. I've spoken to each of you about this in individual therapy and suggested you read Martha Stout's book, *The Sociopath Next Door.* Many of your husbands and ex's have symptoms of this disorder, even if they don't quite meet the diagnosis. Do you want to share your stories about this today?

Sharon: Please remind me what a sociopath is. I keep getting it mixed up with a psychopath and a narcissist.

Pat: This can seem a bit confusing, because antisocial personality disorder, sociopathic personality disorder and psychopathic personality disorder refer to the same chronic mental health condition. Sociopaths are more dangerous than narcissists because they have no regard for right and wrong and often disregard the rights, wishes, and feelings of others.

Many symptoms of these two disorders overlap, but someone with sociopathic personality disorder has no awareness of, or regard for, other people's feelings. They have no remorse for their hurtful actions. They are often adept and accurate in perceiving how other people think, but with no real understanding or regard for feelings. Men are at greater risk for sociopathic personality disorder than women. The Diagnostic and Statistical Manual of Psychological Diagnoses (DSM V) says sociopaths are 3% of the male population and 1% of the female population.

If you're dealing with sociopathic disorder, you're likely to see verbal and physical abuse, lying, reckless behavior, risky sexual behavior, conning or lying to others, and feeling no remorse or justifying behavior after harming others. And that's just a start. They often steal, vandalize, are violent, show cruelty to animals, and are bullying and violent toward people in their lives. Anyone who's involved with a sociopathic person should be educated about this mental health condition and receive counseling to help set boundaries and protect oneself from the aggression, violence, cruelty, and anger. Sociopaths will abuse those closest to them by psychologically and emotionally abusing, controlling finances, sexually abusing, and physically abusing. I'm going to show you a list of abusive behavior that can occur when you're involved with a sociopath.

The abuse can be physical, psychological, emotional, financial, and sexual. (Power and Control: Definitions of Domestic Abuse, page 261).

Pat: Renee, can you tell us about your husband's abusive behavior?

Renee: Okay. Besides the whole prostitution stuff, hundreds of little incidents with pathological lying, narcissism, and sociopathic behaviors all combined to make me think I was going crazy. It could be an everyday thing, like driving the car over my newly seeded lawn, or it could happen at a special event, like when my son performed in a concert downtown with his school choir. That should have been a magical family event, but my husband refused to sit with me and our other kids. He sat a few rows away. He gave no reason for this and no prior warning that anything was bothering him. I spent the concert trying not to cry. I told the kids their father just needed space.

Another time, we attended a gala opening downtown. I wore a beautiful new chiffon skirt and sequined top. I don't get dressed up often, so I was excited about feeling pretty and sparkly that night. My husband stood behind me in the buffet line, but when I reached the end and turned around, he was gone. I thought perhaps he was in the men's room, so I stood near the end of the table waiting for him to come back. Eventually I sat on a bench right there and ate dinner because I didn't want to miss him when he came back for me. I kept looking for him amid hundreds of people. Two hours later—I'm not making this up—he came up to me and said I wrecked his evening because he couldn't find me. He said I didn't even know how to properly go out in public. He spoke harshly, took me home in silence, and drove off after I left the car. I cried a lot that night. So many other times when I thought we'd have a nice date night, he would turn it into a disaster. Can I give another example? I don't want to monopolize the session.

Debbie: We learn from each other. Go ahead.

Renee: Once when my daughter was in the hospital for several days recovering from severe mono, my ex took apart my home computer where I had all my work. My son called to tell me computer parts were scattered all over our bedroom floor. When I called my husband to ask what the heck he was doing, he said he was trying to "clean" the computer. He has no computer training to do such a thing, and had no idea what he was doing. Fortunately, my daughter was dating a computer whiz at the time, and she asked him if he could salvage my files. Her boyfriend took the parts to his house and came back with a rebuilt computer. He said it took him hours and hours. I was so grateful. This was my computer. My ex had his own computer at his office, so he had no reason to touch mine. My sister told me he was trying to wreck my job.

Pat: These are great examples of how a sociopath treats others. Also, your husband was gas lighting you—trying to make you think you were the crazy one. Sharon, what about your husband?

Sharon: My husband often calls me crazy. He says I don't make any sense when I tell him he's too controlling about money or dictating what I wear or who I have as friends. He figured out a way to tap into my phone system so he knows when I use it and who I talk to. I found cameras hidden around our house screening my behavior at home. When I asked him about it, he told me he put the cameras in place to watch our babysitters. We hardly ever have babysitters. That was a lie. Sometimes when I'm at the gym he shows up in the middle of the day, just to see if I'm there. I see him lurking in the background at parties watching my conversations. He gets creepier all the time, so it's good to have a name for this: sociopathic personality disorder. I didn't know executives could be sociopaths. I'm going to read more about it.

Pat: Actually, many successful, accomplished men—and women— are sociopaths. People around them sometimes think the behavior means they're super confident and their lack of emotion is businesslike. These people get away with cruel, obnoxious behavior at work and at home. Occupations that attract the most sociopaths are politics, law, and executive positions. Often they own a business so they don't have to work for anyone else. They can be anywhere, and you may find them entrenched in a bureaucracy where they create their own little kingdoms. The movie and book *Gone Girl* highlight a female sociopath.

Sharon: That sounds right. My husband fires a lot of people, but he makes sure to send huge gift baskets to everyone for Christmas to make a show of being generous. He always buys me diamonds on my birthday and tells people at work about it. I know because his colleagues come up to me at the annual holiday party and ask to see his latest gift. Of course I always have to wear the new necklace that night. My life is one big lie.

Pat: The lying, conniving, sneaking, surveillance, and sabotage are all part of a sociopathic personality. The showiness is narcissism. The two go together in many cases. I want to make sure you all know about the aggression and cruelty of sociopaths: they feel no remorse. These are the kind of men who can hold a baby chipmunk in a bucket of water until it drowns. That's a true story I heard from another woman who married a sociopath. They will push you up against a wall, throw you out a window, or rape you. No remorse. Your tears and suffering mean nothing to them, because they don't have feelings for you.

You've shared the domestic abuse you suffered at the hands of these men. It is never, NEVER, okay to have someone physically or sexually assault you. A push, grabbing you, blocking the door so you can't leave the room—these things are considered domestic abuse, and they are done because these men seek power and control over you. The same with forced sex of any kind. They like to feel they own you.

Stephanie: I remember my husband pushing and shoving me a lot. I finally called 911 when he pinned me against a wall and had his hands around my throat. I'm so glad I finally managed to get away from him. This conversation is scaring me.

Renee: My ex would often come home while I was asleep and force himself sexually on me. I didn't know if this was rape, but it sure felt like it. I remember another thing. When our marriage was in its death throes, he bragged that I couldn't even tell when he was lying. That made me shudder. He was obviously right. I couldn't tell he was lying because I didn't think my husband would ever lie to me. I believed everything he said to me during our marriage.

Pat: Pathological lying is part of the mix. Again, no remorse. It's all part of the game.

Renee: It was a game for him, wasn't it? I was his swat toy. And then there was his parting shot at me.

Debbie: What?

Renee: He said people thought he was leaving me because I had small breasts.

Debbie: What? He's a total creep. And by the way, you are a lovely woman.

Stephanie: He's an asshole. My husband tells me no one else will ever want me.

Debbie: You are an incredible woman, Stephanie, and you are still young. Ditch this guy.

Sharon: What cruelty. Is there a pill to cure this?

Pat: No, and as I said before, psychotherapy can't help them. A personality disorder is really a character disorder, and there's no cure. Rarely will these men participate in real therapy, although they may pretend. They don't want to change and don't think they need help.

When dealing with a sociopathic personality, family members need to seek treatment. Everyone involved with the person should learn about the symptoms. Families need help learning to set boundaries and protect themselves from the aggression, violence, and anger common to the sociopath. After a divorce from one of these guys, have as little contact as possible with him.

Reader: Being with a sociopath sounds dangerous. How do women get away from these men?

Session Twenty

The Serial Cheater

Pat: Last week we talked about sociopaths and their dangerous behavior. Infidelity is a common symptom of your husbands' disorders. Debbie and Renee had husbands who cheated on them with multiple women. Debbie, you suspected cheating and then hired a private investigator. Why?

Debbie: Cheater was even more absent than usual, but I noticed he took more trouble with his appearance all of a sudden. A couple of times he stayed out all night and said he was working. Like Renee's husband, he said he was always at work or out with a supplier working hard for the family, so I should leave him alone and stop nagging.

Pat: Was it your expectation that he wouldn't see other women?

Debbie: Of course.

Pat: Some people have open marriages, so I wanted to make sure. How did the infidelity make you feel?

Debbie: I was hurt. I felt betrayed, and I couldn't understand why he was doing it. I felt rejected.

Stephanie: I feel awful that my husband is now dating his secretary.

Renee: I felt rejected too, and it happened so early in my marriage--my husband probably had no intention of being faithful at all. I think he lied right at the altar. We had a recommitment ceremony when our fourth child was baptized, yet he was cheating on me through all that. After my marriage blew up from his gonorrhea bomb, he said, "All men cheat and we think about sex every seven seconds." He also said, "All men watch porn, so what's your problem?"

Sharon: I wonder if my husband, who's evidently a narcissist and sociopath, has cheated on me. He's away so much on business and when he comes home he wants me to wear slinky clothes to events and get a Brazilian wax. He's always trying to make me sexier, especially when we're going out in public. He selects what I'm going to wear. I may be fooling myself to think he's been faithful.

Pat: Knowing if your husband is unfaithful isn't always easy. I often find that men who accuse their wives of infidelity and track their phones are actually the ones who are cheating. They project infidelity onto their wives as a type of defense mechanism for their own behavior. So, I can't tell you, Sharon, that your husband is unfaithful, but if I was a betting person, I'd wager he's seeing other women. A husband who insists on questioning and drilling you about infidelity is probably cheating on you.

Debbie, you hired a private investigator and found out your husband was meeting with a woman at a motel, and Renee, you were told to get checked for gonorrhea. These were direct reality checks. For many other women, like Sharon, the situation is less clear, but they have a gut feeling about distrusting their husbands.

Reader: This has been quite an education about men who are liars, cheats, and creeps. I hope other women will realize they don't need to stay with these men. I wonder when you start facing the truth?

Facing the Truth

Session Twenty-One

Breaking the Silence and Razing the Façade

Pat: Hi everybody. Tonight I'd like to let Stephanie talk about her recent experiences in court.

Stephanie: I don't know if anyone else feels this way, but I can't stand having my personal problems aired in a public courtroom. During this latest visit to court I had to hear three other couples argue before my case was called. I wanted to crawl under the table. But my restraining order would expire if I didn't get it continued.

Sharon: Going public is definitely one of my concerns. Only my family and one close friend know my marriage is in trouble.

Debbie: I agree it feels weird talking about personal matters in front of strangers, but my perspective is that going public, especially in a court, gives us protection. Keeping things quiet protects your husband who battered you, Stephanie. Going to court creates a public record of what happened. You need to convince the judge how violent your husband is, and that his behavior is awful, not yours.

Renee: I was anxious when I first went to court, especially when I actually recognized one of the other couples in the courtroom. That felt awkward and embarrassing, but I managed to push down those feelings. Even worse was being in the same room with my ex. I never looked at him, and I always went to court with my sisters or a friend. Debbie even went with me once.

Debbie: Yes, that was an interesting day in court for sure. I stood right in front of you when he was walking down the hallway being a loud jerk. My own court dates were usually bizarre because my ex, through his lawyer, lied about everything. For me, it was harder and embarrassing to tell my whole family what was going on in my marriage—especially my father who got along well with my husband. They all thought I had a great family. When they found out the details of the cheating, drinking, insults, disrespect, lies, and stress, my father and my family completely supported me. My dad wanted to punch him in the nose.

On the other hand, Cheater's family thinks I'm a shrew, and that is painful because I once had a good relationship with his mother. He told his family what he wanted them to believe, so I shouldn't be surprised. The kids also have to deal with having our family troubles out in public. My two daughters didn't want me to tell the school, but I had to let the school know in case they saw my kids struggling or having behavior problems. I promised my kids I'd ask the school to keep the information private, and they went along with that.

Pat: That's a good suggestion, Debbie. And I agree that parents of school age kids should let the school know about a divorce or pending divorce. Usually the school notices a change in the children's academics and maybe their behavior. A school counselor, a favorite teacher, or a coach can be important sounding boards for your children. Once the divorce is final, the school records must be updated so bulletins and notices go to both parents, if you have joint legal custody.

The divorce also has fallout with family gatherings. What are your experiences with that?

Renee: My kids had good times with their cousins on the other side of the family, and fortunately they still contact each other online to keep in touch. I have no idea who knows what. I'm worried things will be awkward for my kids at funerals or weddings, but that's a consequence of how their father behaved.

Stephanie: My family has been great. My parents drove from New Hampshire to help me during that first awful week. I have a sister who lives not far away. My husband's family is all from this area, and they hate me. They all think I'm wrecking the family and screwing up their grandchildren. As I mentioned before, they're all heavy drinkers and only see what they want to see. His mother told me I was awful to go to court and tell lies about her son.

Pat: Stephanie, alcoholics usually blame the people around them for their drinking and all their troubles. They will blame anyone but themselves. And your alcoholic in-laws who have an alcoholic son undergoing a divorce will be in strong denial. Please consider going to Al Anon and having your boys attend Al-Teen. That will help you detach from taking their scorn personally. This is NOT about you.

Stephanie: Maybe.

Renee: Stephanie, I'll go to Al Anon with you to start with, if it makes you more comfortable.

Stephanie: Thanks, Renee. Maybe.

Renee: When I got to court I felt going public was both for my protection and an act of defiance.

Pat: What do you mean by defiance?

Renee: On that night my ex told me I should go to a doctor to get tested for gonorrhea, he also told me I couldn't tell anyone. It's like he wanted to shame me and make me part of what he did.

Pat: You're right, Renee. He was trying to shame you and make you part of his dirty little secrets. It's much like a child molester who tells children they need to keep the molesting a secret. But, as with children who are molested, it's important to speak up and say something about what happened to you. You need to break the silence in order to not take on the shame, and you need to make the perpetrator accountable for his behavior. Speaking up is vital!

Renee: When he told me about the gonorrhea, I felt like a bomb went off in the room, because it was so sudden, so unexpected and so cataclysmic to my brain. I followed him downstairs yelling "how could you do this?" He just sat on the couch stone faced, ignoring me.

I marched back upstairs and sat at the computer where it all began a few minutes earlier. Right then, I wrote an email telling my sisters what just happened. None of my family lives around me, and I needed them to know right away. I was afraid he might kill me, so I added to the email that having sex with a prostitute was not a mistake. Buying sex from a prostitute isn't like ordering a regular coffee and getting a decaf instead. He didn't mistake the prostitute for me! Buying a prostituted woman was a decision he made, certainly not a mistake. As an afterthought, I added his sisters and his mother as recipients to the email. Then I pressed *Send*.

Pat: Why did you do that?

Renee: Sending an email defied what he said I couldn't do. I had nothing to be ashamed of. I think he counted on me being ashamed that I might have gonorrhea, or I couldn't satisfy "my man." The fact that I tested positive for gonorrhea showed that he was still having sex with me—regularly. I just did not know this man any more. And he apparently didn't know me at all if he thought I'd cover his behavior.

Pat: When did you let others know?

Renee: Over the next few days and weeks, I told some good friends exactly what he did and that I tested positive for the gonorrhea he brought into my life. I also spoke with my pastoral advisor. I didn't want to go through this alone. I spread the word to a few people at work and a few neighbors, telling them I was going through a divorce and he was involved in prostitution right there in our neighborhood. One of my friends is married to a cop and I wanted at least one policeman to know all about this in case anything happened to me. I also told a friend who's a newspaper reporter, just in case. I had many offers of safe houses or people who would come over on a moment's notice. Everything in my world was changing, so anything could happen to me at any time. I needed lots of support and protection.

Pat: What about the children's schools?

Renee: My youngest daughter was still at school, so I called her guidance counselor in case she needed support there. I also told my daughter's doctors and all my doctors. The only thing I feel ashamed of is that I married the bum and he fooled me every day.

Pat: Think of yourselves as each living within many circles. Your nuclear family is the closest circle, then a ring for the extended family, followed by rings of friends, colleagues at work, neighbors, and community. Some people have dozens of people in each circle and some have only a few. You have every right to tell anyone who will help support you. This is completely your call. What is the place of this support group in your circles?

Debbie: I tell everything here!

Stephanie: I do too. I'm glad to know I'm not the only one with a messed up family.

Renee: I haven't told the entire story of the bad stuff throughout my marriage to anyone other than this support group, Pat, and my lawyer.

Sharon: I feel better sharing about my husband's behavior here. I don't have family nearby, although I'm on the phone and email them all the time. Here, I'm with other women who know about bad marriages. Thank you, although I wish I wasn't here. I wish I wasn't a member of this club.

Pat: That's a good way to say it, Sharon, but if you're in this life boat, at least you're not alone.

Reader: Some of these women struggled with having people know what happened in their marriages. Does that mean they blamed themselves on some level, or they feared others would blame them? Maybe they see divorce as a sign of failure.

Session Twenty-Two

Does Divorce Mean I Failed?

Pat: How do you feel about your marriages ending in divorce?

Renee: I feel like a failure. How could I not? My family is the most important thing to me. I failed in marriage, and more importantly, I failed the kids by selecting a terrible man to be their father. If divorce is now the central situation in my life, then my life is defined by failure. I am now a statistic.

Stephanie: I feel depressed that my marriage is crumbling.

Sharon: Me too. I wanted so much to be happily married.

Pat: I want to remind you that you married for love to guys who said they wanted a family. You were lied to and fooled by men with deep personality issues and addictions. I assure you, they don't feel sadness or remorse about getting a divorce, unless their feelings are for show.

Debbie: I feel awful that my kids are struggling with being rejected by their father as he marries a woman he met at a massage parlor.

Pat: How has he rejected them?

111

Debbie: He failed to pay for their support, even though the judge ordered it. He sent Christmas cards for the first few years, and that's all. Now, the kids don't even want to open cards from him. They hate Cheater as much as I do.

Renee: I agree about feeling bad for the kids. Finding out my marriage was an illusion was bad enough. But he also led my kids to believe we had a family, that he was a father. He gave them droplets of attention, but only at public performances and games. We were just a cover for his disgusting life. I didn't see that until the gonorrhea bomb, so I feel like I failed my kids. I feel terrible that I was gullible enough to marry and have four children with this creep. The most important thing in my life was to have a happy family. My kids deserved better, but I blew it. That is on me.

Pat: Renee, do your kids have a relationship with your ex?

Renee: There is no relationship. For a year or so he sent Christmas and birthday cards. Then that stopped. They don't want anything to do with a lying, cheating, narcissistic, sex addict who spent more time with prostitutes than with them. I feel the guilt of having selected this monster to be their father. I try to make up for it by being attentive and buying them stuff.

Pat: All kids in a divorce need extra attention from loving parents, but you aren't going to solve your guilt with presents. You all need to keep reassuring your kids that your love is solid. All you can do is go forward. You're sorry for the past, and you can tell them that. Keep assuring them of your love and look forward to being their mom. The past is not in your control, only the future.

On the broader subject of feeling like failures, I want you to start thinking about divorce not as a failure, but as an acknowledgment that you can have a better life ahead for yourself and your kids. I want you to begin seeing yourselves as courageous heroines who are taking a brave and important step toward a healthier life for yourself and your families.

Sharon: That's interesting.

Reader: The marriages were bad. Divorce is always tough, and life afterward will hold challenges, but you have to be brave about taking that first courageous step.

Session Twenty-Three

How Can I Survive Financially?

Pat: Let's talk about financial survival tonight. You've all either taken the action step filing for divorce, or you're considering that step Making a plan is part of taking action and will help you be less fearful. Sharon expressed concern about how she'll survive financially, since she isn't working outside the home. Money is a big issue for her. What about the rest of you?

Debbie: I had to divide the business; actually he got the whole business, and there was a complicated payment schedule to me, and then I'm out. I got the house. Divorce depletes your wealth and kind of diminishes your self-worth too. And lawyers are expensive. I admire people who can come to a settlement through mediation or even by themselves. I received full title to the house in the divorce, and he got the business, but he owes me money for the business and he owes child support.

Stephanie: We don't have a lot of money as a couple, but my husband's family has money. If they bankroll him I don't have a chance on a fair settlement.

Debbie: That's not true, Stephanie. Think about what you need, be clear about it, and stick to it.

Stephanie: I think we'll have to sell the house, and I hate that. My kids will hate me for it too.

Renee: You can ask the judge to let you have the house as part of your settlement. You'll need an appraisal. But even if you end up having to sell the house and divide the proceeds, think about living without a drunken husband who calls you a stupid b---- all the time. Your daily life would have to get better, even in a small apartment. It will be your place where you feel safe. My youngest daughter wants me to stay in our house, even though it has a lot of bad memories for me. After I got all my ex-husband's crap out my sisters came over and rearranged the furniture so the place would look different. I was sort of frozen looking at how empty the house seemed. Pat told me I was clearing out my ex and decluttering my life. I'm now on a tight budget, but in a strange way, being poor is worth it. I have a sign over my desk at home that says, "All I have is all I need."

Sharon: I still dread the possibility of losing my house and my kids.

Pat: There are no grounds for you to lose your kids.

Debbie: Get a good lawyer who can help you deal with a man as manipulative as your husband. It may not be simple or easy to divorce, but eventually this will end and you'll be free of him.

Renee: Your feelings, Sharon, are very understandable to me. I felt like I was standing on the edge of a cliff. I was a stay at home mom for about five years of our marriage after the kids were born. Then I worked only part time, between ten and twenty hours a week. I worked at home a lot. I was afraid the divorce would make me homeless, but I ended up with the house and part of his pension, plus all the furniture and stuff I got from my family or bought myself.

Does anyone here ever read Dear Abby in the newspaper? She tells women, "Figure out if you're better off with him or without him." Well, I tried to factor in values for my health, peace of mind and safety. Once I understood what he was doing to me and the kids, the greater number was clearly to get out of the marriage as fast as possible. I'm not saying it wasn't hard. I got used to having nice furniture, and I always used the part time salary from my tax work as my spending money. Now my salary is essential for paying bills, with nothing left over for luxuries. On the other hand, I no longer have to see his face and hear his lies. Peace is priceless.

Debbie: I also suggest you ask for whatever help you need. Friends and even neighbors helped me with home tasks, because I didn't know how to fix anything. Instead of going out to a restaurant, now a couple of my friends often just get together to watch a movie at someone's house. At first I worried that being less secure financially meant I was being selfish and it would hurt my kids. Now I see my divorce as a learning opportunity for everyone to pull together as a family and make do with less. I've also learned to accept help and my kids went on vacations with their friends' families for a while. I went to tag sales for stuff, and we go to a bargain place for haircuts. It's all fine.

Pat: I really like hearing you talk about how to live more simply and find happiness in the sheer ability to live peacefully and on your own. This reminds me of two quotes by the wonderful, wise Maya Angelou: "We need much less than we think." and "I've learned that making a living is not the same thing as making a life."

I also suggest you count your blessings at least once every single day. Seriously, make a list of your riches, even if they aren't financial. Many divorced women tell me they actually feel more secure financially because they don't continually worry about their ex's wasting money on frivolous things. These women are now in charge, and they handle their own finances wisely and well. You are all accomplished women with good educations and great children. You will survive, and ultimately thrive.

Reader: Just when these women feel hurt, angry, and alone, they have to worry about how to survive financially. Divorce is almost like a death in the family.

Session Twenty-Four

Grieving the Marriage You Hoped For

Pat: Last session we talked about the financial fallout of a divorce. I want to check in with how you're doing.

Sharon: I want to announce that I told my husband to leave last weekend. More and more I've been feeling I can't go on being his little puppet. When I asked him to leave the house, he told me he didn't have to go. Then he started to get nasty and scary, coming at me, so I picked up the phone and called the police. They came and told my husband to leave the house. So he's out for now. He went to a hotel or maybe his office. I talked with a lawyer to help me understand what a divorce would mean for me and my kids, and I'm making a lot of lists. I think our meeting last week helped me feel I can manage the finances on my own. Although I'm scared and find it hard to concentrate, I think I also feel relieved about making this decision.

Debbie: Sharon, good for you!

Renee: Congratulations, Sharon! I know this is huge for you. I'm glad you decided not to stay with a guy who's such a control freak and abuser. We're all here to help you get through this.

Sharon: Thanks. It's scary, but I am starting to feel different already—like a weight is lifting.

Renee: Yes, that's how I felt when my ex finally got out of the house.

Debbie: We've been through this and we'll be here for you.

Stephanie: I'm happy for you, Sharon, but I feel low right now. It's hard to be positive about anything. I'm scared about money and sometimes just sad that my marriage is ending. Even though I know divorce is what I need to do, it's still hard. I guess I'm grieving for the marriage I hoped for when we were newlyweds. He was so passionate then. I've been writing to help me through this and face the facts. Can I read what I wrote?

Renee: That would be great, Stephanie. I find writing helps so much.

Debbie: I'd love to hear what you wrote.

Pat: I'm so glad you're getting your thoughts out on paper. Please read it for us.

Stephanie: Okay, here goes. I call it "I Am Not the First."

I am not the first, and certainly not the last woman who fell in love with her soul mate and her worst enemy. But as I look to the unknown future, I am both fearful and second guessing my decision to go through with a divorce from my husband for the sake of myself and my children. Loving someone who loves and hates with equal passion casts a brilliant, intoxicating light upon me that takes my breath away. Yet it also conceals an inconceivable darkness that lurks beneath the surface. The verbal and emotional abuse became so overwhelming that I can no longer stay with him and survive mentally and emotionally and be the person I need to be as a mother. Everything in life has equal opposites, and my story is no different. Life's choices that don't work out as planned can become life's greatest learning lessons instead of our greatest regrets—so I am told by wise women. I need to take back my power and move toward a better future for my family even if it holds uncertainty and fear, because only by moving forward in spite of these emotions will I have a real future.

Renee: Incredible—so good. Now we're both crying!

Debbie: Wow! That is so well put. I love it. Great job, Stephanie.

Pat: You described so well the emotional states of love and hate. Both of them are the most intense feelings on the emotional spectrum. However, in a healthy marriage you don't have both poles. You do not both love and hate your partner. In dysfunctional relationships these extremes often exist. When you feel hate for someone, I don't believe you can truly be feeling love for them.

Sharon: It's sad, too. We all hoped for much more. I'm still reeling from my decision to ask my husband to leave. I feel good and bad at the same time. I need to adjust to it.

Renee: Getting used to being on your own can take quite a while. For me, I'm adapting to life as a single working woman with my daughter at home and my other kids grown up. I think all of us are still hurting, even though two years have passed since my divorce became final. And the divorce itself dragged on for over two years. To be honest, I still feel awful about the marriage, but then I remember my marriage was an illusion. Then I get mad at myself, and then I try to think about something else.

Pat: Grieving about the marriage you thought you had is perfectly understandable. You loved the "what ifs" and "could have beens." Sometimes reality stinks. Women sometimes deal with the sudden death of a loving husband, but you are all dealing with the death of your hopes and dreams. I know it's hard.

Debbie: Do we go through the stages of grief?

Pat: The famous Kubler-Ross stages of grief don't occur in exact order, but in general I would say, yes—you will go through stages of grief. You'll deal with sadness, denial, anger, and then more of the same. You'll bargain with yourself that you can make it better, and finally you'll accept what you need to do as you move on and become healthy. Adjusting to a life without your husbands will take time, no matter how awful they were. And remember when you feel sad, it isn't necessarily about missing him; rather you're missing the life you hoped for and dreamed you'd have with him. Ultimately you'll come to accept the loss of your marriage.

Debbie: I had a party when my divorce decree became final.

Stephanie: Were you that happy?

Debbie: Not exactly happy—it was more like relief and freedom, and I wanted to mark the occasion with people I cared about. I even found divorce party invitations. Mostly it was a thank-you party for people who supported me, and I wanted love and laughter in my house again.

Renee: I remember that party, and you had lots of people there. As for me, I feel relieved and grateful to be away from my ex, but no party for me. I really, really thought I'd be married to one man for the rest of my life. Did he ever love me? No. He never loved me! I think I was in shock for a long time. For a while, I noticed every different thing—like doing less laundry and having his stuff suddenly absent from the house, and only one car in the driveway. Don't get me wrong; I recognize my marriage was an illusion and I was married to a sick, narcissistic, sociopathic, lying creep. So what I still need now is quiet. The recovery is taking more time than I expected, but I feel better than I did last year. I hope I'm not wallowing in self- pity. I realize many women are in dire straits after a divorce.

Pat: Be gentle with yourselves. Deciding to divorce, getting a divorce, and life after the divorce are all ruptures in the lives you were planning. Mending takes time. Push yourself to gradually get out there and experience life.

Reader: I didn't realize that even when divorce is the right thing to do, it still brings lingering sadness.

Session Twenty-Five

News Flash: Everyone Knew But You, Even the Kids

Pat: Did any of you have to deal with people being shocked that your marriage was in trouble?

Stephanie: That's a funny question.

Pat: Why?

Stephanie: I've been living in ignorance. No one was shocked, surprised, or saddened by my decision to separate. Everyone seems to be telling me to get the divorce. I found that shocking at first. But even though much of his behavior was saved for inside our walls at home, apparently everyone knew about his alcoholism and horrible behavior toward me. All along, I thought I did a good job hiding it. When I went out with my husband, my attitude was, "My marriage isn't that hard to deal with. I can handle it." Good thing I'm not a spy, because my face is apparently like an open book.

Pat: It's not uncommon for the people around you see what you've been trying not to see.

Stephanie: I was at my son's game one night last week, and one of the dad's commented to me that I looked happy. I asked him what he meant, and he said I never smiled and always looked stressed when my husband was around.

Pat: Why do you think your family and friends are giving you advice, and what are they telling you to do?

Stephanie: It seems like everyone's saying the same thing: divorce him. I'm getting bombarded with comments from my sister and parents that they never liked him and he's no good. I had no idea they felt that way. Now they tell me they've been waiting for me to wake up, because of his drinking and swearing all the time. My sister told me she once wanted to punch him when he called me a stupid b----, but she didn't because he was my husband.

Pat: What about you, Debbie? Did your family or friends know before you did that your marriage was over?

Debbie: My parents seemed to like Cheater at first. After we had children, from time to time they'd ask, "Where's your husband? He's never around." I used to cover his absences by saying he was tied up at work. The kids didn't have much of a relationship with him, because he stayed away. When the big break up came and I was crying a lot, both kids made it clear they wanted nothing to do with him. When he called they hung up on him. He was reaping what he sowed.

Renee: For me, people said they were shocked I stayed married so long. And that was before anyone knew about his sexploits and the gonorrhea bomb. My sisters barely tolerated my ex. My friends didn't seem comfortable around him. I often got invitations not as a couple, but just for me to go out with the girls. People treated me as a single woman long before the divorce. When I first announced I was getting a divorce, the most common reactions were "You're better off without him" and "Finally!"

I was surprised to find out most people considered him a jerk. Not only that, I learned that people close to me had watched me change into a person they liked less. I guess I didn't smile much either. I got an earful after I filed for the divorce. I sometimes wonder what people at his work knew about his philandering, his porn habit, and buying prostitutes.

Pat: Your children are older, Renee. Did they know you should divorce before you did?

Renee: When they were young they loved any attention they got from him, but he never stayed home to hang out with the family. He gave them droplets of attention—just barely enough. He never got on the floor and played with them when they were little. I think my kids were completely shocked at what he did with prostitutes, but not surprised I would divorce him. They felt the tension in the house. My daughter told me Christmases were always especially terrible, while I thought I was doing a good job pretending everyone was having a good time. I gasped when she told me that. I'm so sorry they didn't have a good childhood, and they knew what was going on. They saw I was walking on egg shells and they heard him always belittling me and walking out the door.

Sharon: My mother told me she wasn't surprised when I first called to tell her about the separation. She was a little taken aback that he got physical with me, but she could see how controlling he'd become. When she told him once to relax around the kids, he snapped at her that he didn't need her advice how to be a father. She didn't say much to him after that. I have one close friend who said she'd do anything to help me get out of the marriage. She said she can't stand my husband. That was a surprise to me. As for my sister-in-law, I can hear her saying "I told you so." Now I feel motivated to get the divorce, because I know it's not just me.

Stephanie: Everyone around me seems to think there isn't any hope. I need their support, but I can't be rushed. I still have hope. My sons are angry at me, and probably at him too. I've never asked them if they think I should continue with the divorce.

Pat: We can talk more about your sons later, but it's best not to ask them what you should do. Listen to your family and friends who now tell you what they really think about your husbands—and it's not good. People who love you do not like him. They witness that he doesn't bring out the best in you. When most of the people you care about don't like the person you married, that's another sign you're in an unhealthy relationship. They've probably been biting their tongues for a long time, but once you announced the divorce or separation, they're eager to help you push him out.

Reader: Love really is blind.

Session Twenty-Six

I'm Still Afraid to Leave

Pat: How is everyone doing? Sharon, you look pretty tense.

Sharon: Yeah, give me a few minutes.

Stephanie: I need to talk. I keep having the same issue over and over. It's money. My son Jay says he needs special soccer shorts with padding on them. These shorts cost $38.00, so I tell him to ask his father. His father tells him that he has no money because I kicked him out and that he gives all his money to me, so Jay has to ask me. I then tell Jay I don't have enough for the bills, and to please see if he can do without. Then Jay yells that he can't stand it and storms out of the house. I feel responsible for the whole family being miserable.

Pat: Your husband is trying to portray you as selfish and not caring about the family. He's trying to make your boys angry at you and create a wedge between you and your sons. Remember, you are not being selfish. You are trying to live a sane life.

Stephanie: I know, but it's so hard to be blamed by my sons and my husband.

Renee: Stephanie, I know it is hard right now, but you'll feel a lot better when you can start setting boundaries with your husband. Please stop thinking this is your fault. You were an abused woman taking a very brave step to get away from an abuser.

Sharon: I get what Stephanie means. It's hard to take the final step of divorcing. I'm now trying to get on with my life and get the divorce started. My husband is angry one day about my decision to have him leave, and the next day he's crying and saying he cannot live without me. He keeps flip-flopping, which is confusing for me.

Pat: I'm sure that's incredibly frustrating, Sharon. But remember your husband is two faced and will try to manipulate you to get back with him so he can regain control over you. Please keep track of any threats or concerns you have. Keep a small notebook handy. If you feel threatened by him in any way, call the police. Some guys are superb actors and fool a lot of people. I'm glad he's out of your house.

Sharon: When he called today, he was ranting. He said he checked out the lawyer I was talking to, and I will get nothing if I divorce him. He plans to fight for the kids too, and he said he has the money to hire the best lawyer around. And then he said if he can't have me, no one will. My mother came to stay with me for a while and that makes me feel safer.

Pat: Write everything down and tell your lawyer. These are threats. Your husband is a piece of work, Sharon. He violates all kinds of boundaries. He must know you see me in therapy because he invited me to join his LinkedIn network. I totally ignored his request.

Sharon: Oh, God! I feel like he's chasing me and knows where I go and who I talk to. I don't know if he's in the parking lot right now. I feel like a hunted dog. He uses the "find my phone" app on the Iphone to see where I am. Then he texts me asking why I'm there. He's also constantly tracking me on Mint.com to check credit card expenses on a daily basis.

Pat: So he's following you and trying to intimidate you. He's used to getting his way. He's a bully, Sharon, and not likely to change. Maybe you can get a restraining order that specifically requires him to stop all this surveillance. Does he have the kids now?

Sharon: No, thank God. My kids are with my mom at my house.

Pat: That's good. Call the police and report any and all threats from him. We will walk you to your car. Most bully's skulk away when they're outnumbered. Your husband is unpredictable. Call your lawyer and explain everything you just told us here. I hope your Mom can stay with you for the time being.

Sharon: What am I going to do? I hate this.

Debbie: You are a smart, strong, woman, and you can and should divorce him. He's trying to intimidate you into backing down.

Sharon: I am intimidated. I'm afraid of him and afraid for my children.

Renee: Pat, why is Sharon's husband acting like this? Would he really hurt her?

Pat: I don't know what he might do. I do know that the more you stand up for yourself, Sharon, the more he'll try to push you down. You threaten him by being a strong woman. He has been in control of you for a long time, and he's becoming more and more threatened by losing that control. The reason for the abuse is to regain power and control over you—it shows he's losing his grip.

I've said it before: the only thing worse than divorcing an abuser is staying married to one. And let me add further, the only thing worse than divorcing a sociopath is staying married to one. Please take precautions by locking your doors and using an alarm system. Don't hesitate to call the police if you feel threatened in any way. If he's following you, call the police and tell your lawyer. Surround yourself with support. It's good your mother is with you.

Reader: If love is blind, then it seems like fear also makes us blind.

It's Over! I'm Done!

Session Twenty-Seven

The "Aha" Moment: I Deserve Better than This

Pat: Last session was intense. Sharon, will you update us on how you're doing this week?

Sharon: I made it here. When I left the last session my husband was sitting in his car down the street. I called the cops. Two policemen came and talked to me, then went to his car and talked to him again. My mom was freaking out.

The police said they'd warn my husband to stay away from me and told me to go to court for a restraining order. So the next day I was in court. I couldn't believe what the judge said. She said that divorce is stressful on both parties, and she warned my husband to "behave." That's the word she used, like he was a child. His lawyer asked the judge not to issue a restraining order, and gave a story about how much stress he's under. The judge went with that. My husband texted me in the hall right after court: "You can't win."

Debbie: That's awful. Did you show the text to your lawyer?

Sharon: Yeah, I did. She told me to be careful, and to ask the police to keep an extra watch on my house.

Debbie: Do you feel safe?

Sharon: No, not really. My mom is still with me.

Pat: Sometimes the court system doesn't go exactly as we hoped. I think your husband is an extreme sociopath, Sharon, who knows exactly how to manipulate the court system and even his attorney. I'm often disappointed that judges don't seem to understand sociopathic behavior. Is your husband getting any counseling?

Sharon: His lawyer said in court he was seeing a counselor, but who knows? He may have made that up for the judge. Now I don't want to talk anymore. I just want to listen.

Pat: Sure, Sharon. Just sit and be with us tonight. Stephanie, you emailed me yesterday that you have some news.

Stephanie: Yes, I want to announce that my lawyer filed for my divorce.

Debbie: Congratulations!

Renee: You made a decision. How do you feel?

Pat: What made you decide to go forward with divorce?

Stephanie: Well, I suppose there are a lot of reasons with all the drinking and abuse. But it came down to his phone call to me a few days ago. He'd been drinking, and he was raging about my lawyer sending him a letter about overdue bills that he was supposed to pay according to our separation agreement. He shouted about how he is broke and it's all my fault and on and on, always ending with, "You stupid b----."

I hung up on him and told myself, "Wow, I haven't heard him yelling at me for about three days. I don't want to live like that again. I want those few days of not being yelled at to become every day not being yelled at." A lightbulb went on in my head that there is no realistic hope for the marriage. My lawyer asked if I was ready, because he'll probably howl when he gets the divorce complaint. I told her—"Yes!" She said she's been ready with the papers for a long time.

Pat: It's great that you know how good it feels to have even a few days of peace. I agree with your lawyer: now that you've filed things may get worse before they get better. But it will get better. When did he get served with divorce papers?

Stephanie: Today. This morning or afternoon.

Debbie: Oh my gosh. Really?

Stephanie: Yeah. I'm pretty nervous about this. I feel kind of giddy and terrified at the same time. I wanted it to be on a day I had Group so I could get some support. So I told my lawyer to have it happen today.

Debbie: Give me a hug.

Renee: Me too.

Sharon: We have to be brave.

Pat: We're all here for you. And through tough times ahead we will continue to be here for each other. You just took a courageous step, Stephanie and you too, Sharon. Let's find out from the divorced ladies what it was like at the beginning. Debbie, what happened to you when you served your husband with divorce papers?

Debbie: I didn't. He beat me to it. We both had attorneys, and he knew I was getting ready to file. So I was the one who opened my front door to get served. It was pretty awful. It felt like he kicked me. One of my daughters was home.

Renee: What did you do then?

Debbie: I called my lawyer, told her what had happened, and made an appointment. She said it doesn't really matter who files the divorce complaint, but I wish it had been me. I didn't cheat on him.

Renee: I filed against my ex first, but over a year passed after I first met with my lawyer and when I filed for the divorce.

Sharon: Why so long?

Renee: Well, I was seeing Pat in therapy, attending the Al Anon meetings, and then I also started post-traumatic stress therapy. I also saw my ex from time to time, trying to talk things out. That was a waste of energy. Then my brother died, and my ex came rushing in to help me. He said he wanted us to start over. This was a total shocker, but I thought this was good. He even stayed at the house a couple of days, and then he went with me to the memorial service. He also helped me collect and organize my brother's papers when I first went to his house. I was the executrix.

Pat: What happened then?

Renee: The day after my brother's memorial service turned out to be so unbelievably awful. First, let me explain that after the service and the reception the day before, my whole family went to my brother's house. Because I was the executrix, I told everyone to select something that reminded them about my brother. My brother's wife had predeceased him and they had no children. So I would be following his will and distributing everything. I had been at the house already to gather his personal items and his computer. Anyway, that was an emotional day at his house with my whole family, and his wife's family too, and I was pleased when everyone selected items special to them. We shared lots of tears and reminiscing at his house. Later, we ordered pizza. I was exhausted by the time I got back to the hotel.

The next morning when I awakened and sat up in bed, my ex was sitting at the desk in the room, and said he was tired of being my "pool boy," and was embarrassed by my behavior at my brother's house because I was so disorganized. Those were his first words, before I even got out of bed.

I started crying. He said, "There you go again. Boo hoo hoo."

I went next door to my sister's hotel room and she was surprised to see me in my pajamas crying. I asked her if yesterday was awful because of my disorganization. She said, "No, you were amazing, but your husband's a creep." When I drove back to my home, I called my lawyer. We made an appointment, and I told her to let it fly when she was ready.

Stephanie: What happened then?

Renee: I didn't hear from him, but my lawyer forwarded copies of his response from his lawyer. There were a lot of papers—requests, motions, answers, affidavits, financial statements. The paperwork took a long time, but I wanted out of my marriage and to get away from that monster. Finally it was crystal clear for me.

Pat: Why was this your "aha" moment?

Renee: This was actually my second "aha" moment. The first was the gonorrhea bomb. But this time, I couldn't deny that he was, quite simply, an awful person. He wasn't just having a bad day on the ten thousand times he was mean to me. I think I was also moved by my brother who had died. He hated my ex and always wanted me to leave him. So the day after my brother's memorial service, I did.

Reader: It took each of these women a long time to reach the point of filing for divorce. But is that the easy part? And what's a pool boy?

Session Twenty-Eight

I Will Survive Without Him

Pat: Sharon isn't here tonight. She couldn't get a baby sitter, and her mom had to return to her own home in Delaware. Sharon says her mom will come back next week, and she wanted us to know she's fine.

Debbie: I hope so, but I can't imagine she's fine. I worry about her.

Pat: We're all worried about her, but she has a safe house nearby. She also told me her husband was out of the country on business, so she can relax a bit.

So Stephanie, how are you doing?

Stephanie: All hell has broken loose. He got the divorce papers and called each of our boys to tell them what a horrible person I am. He called me too, but I didn't take his call. He left a bunch of voicemails, but I haven't listened to them yet.

Debbie: Save the voicemails and let your lawyer hear them. From now on though, why don't you block him from your phone?

Stephanie: Can I do that?

Debbie: Yes, and you deserve peace and quiet. The lawyers take over now. I'll show you how to block your phone and you can also block your email.

Stephanie: Really?

Renee: Yes. That was important for me. I got calls and emails all the time, until I blocked everything.

Stephanie: I will definitely block my phone and email. Debbie, can you show me later?

Debbie: Absolutely. Happy to do it.

Stephanie: I need a lot of help. I have absolutely no money, not even money for gas.

My lawyer says she'll ask the judge to order him to pay me what he owes, but who knows how long that will take? I'm scared because the bills are piling up.

Renee: What about your paycheck?

Stephanie: I get paid on Friday, thank goodness. I will need every penny for food. I'm worried about my mortgage payment.

Renee: Talk to your lawyer about what to do. Your husband won't cooperate because he wants you to suffer and worry.

Debbie: He's also trying to show you how much you need him.

Stephanie: He may be right. I don't see how I can keep the house on my little salary.

Pat: Stephanie, give it time. Things might settle down in a bit. Often in this transition time things seem the toughest. You might have to eventually sell the house and cut back a lot, and your boys will have to make sacrifices too. They're old enough to understand.

Stephanie: I feel like I'm in hell.

Renee: Here's a little painted stone I keep in my pocket. It says, "If you're going through hell, keep going." Winston Churchill said that. It's your lucky charm now.

Stephanie: Thanks. I need a lucky charm and a lot more.

Debbie: It will get better, I promise. There may be chaos for a while, but you will get through this. And in the meantime, you don't have him calling you names every minute.

Renee: Call and ask your friends and family to help out. Usually people don't know how to help, so be specific. I also had to swallow my pride. My sister had to lend me money to pay some bills and the lawyer's fees. She always treated if we went out for dinner. She even bought my daughter's birthday cake and gifts for her. Everything financial that wasn't essential and routine was frozen during my divorce.

Stephanie: My parents and sister have been great. I wouldn't be able to do anything without them. I just wish this was all over with.

Pat: I've counseled so many women going through their divorces, and men too, and I have yet to see a divorce that doesn't bring out the worst in people. Your husband will not suddenly become a nice, cooperative man during the divorce. He will likely become worse. But YOU will be better in the long run when this is all behind you. Keep moving forward one step at a time. Hold onto your lucky stone!

Reader: Divorce is emotionally and financially draining. It must be tough to do it alone.

Catastrophe

Did your house burn?
Was it flattened by a hurricane?
Shattered by a tornado?
Did lightning strike?

As you sit on a curb where your house once stood,
an EMT asks "Are you okay?"
"No," your voice rasps, "My house is gone."

Then a blanket wraps your shoulders
and a medic gives you oxygen.
A stranger gives you water,
and a friend arrives to hug you.

"You survived" they say with smiles.
"No, I didn't", you cry back, "My soul died today."
"But you are here; you're heart's still beating!" they shout.
You can't bear to hear these words.

But your ears are still hearing,
and your heart is still beating,
and your lungs are still breathing,
and your eyes still see,
and your voice can be heard now, asking for help
to build your new home, where it's safe for you to thrive.

–Renee

Session Twenty-Nine

I May Be Broke; But I'm No Longer Broken

Pat: Let's begin tonight by checking in with everyone.

Stephanie: Where's Sharon?

Pat: I saw her for a session a couple of days ago. Her husband is still out of the country, so she's okay, but she didn't know if she could make it to our session tonight. She has two little kids and no babysitter.

Renee: I'm okay. I've been thinking a lot about you, Stephanie, and the early stages of the divorce.

Debbie: I'm okay too, so let's help Stephanie. I can tell you, that I had a lot more money when I was married. I'm not poor now, but I have to budget, and I can't believe how much money I've spent on legal fees.

Pat: Yes, Debbie, you had a business to divide, besides dividing a household. Your divorce was complicated.

Renee: My salary used to be reserved for my clothes and extras. My husband's salary paid our mortgage and the other bills. Now that I'm living on my paycheck, I've had to cut back a lot. I got the house in the divorce, but now I have to pay the mortgage. My divorce ended in a final

139

settlement. I didn't want alimony, because I didn't want to depend on a monthly check from him. He might get arrested any time trying to buy sex on the street. I wanted him out of my life as much as possible. The settlement came from his pension. It's risky to do it this way, but for me, the sacrifices are worth the peace. I try not to worry about money, but it's always in the back of my mind. I sold my engagement ring to help pay the legal bills. Good riddance. And my entertainment is basically books, TV, and the radio. I go for walks a lot. My one splurge is a gym membership. I take a yoga class that helps me stay together. Pat suggested doing yoga, and it helps. I can also use the equipment at the gym if I feel like doing rigorous exercise. I ride the stationary bike sometimes to release stress.

Pat: Exercise is important to stay healthy—physically and mentally. If you can't afford to pay for a gym membership, you can walk in your neighborhood or do a work out from a TV program. What other advice do you have for Stephanie?

Renee: I haven't bought myself new clothes for quite a while. I didn't much care how I looked for the years it took getting the divorce. I think I wore black pants and a different shirt to work every day for more than two years. I also used scarves to change the look of outfits. Until the divorce was final, I couldn't use my credit card anyway. It was good practice for being poorer.

Debbie: I used to entertain a lot. Cheater wasn't home much, so I often had friends and family over for company, or we went out. Anyway, now I have less company, and I usually ask my guests to bring something. I used to have a cleaning woman. Not anymore. It's different, but being frugal is fine with me. It means I'm free.

Renee: I think I'm much calmer now for my kids at home. The divorce itself is stressful, and I was a basket case for every court appearance, but I kept telling myself it would end soon. I asked a friend or my sisters to come with me for every court appearance. I had anxiety issues being in the same room with him, so I made sure I was never alone at the courthouse. I think I already mentioned that Debbie came with me once.

Stephanie: That's a good idea. My lawyer explained there are steps to go through and a bunch of court appearances. But I'm thinking about trying to mediate my divorce. Did anybody try mediation?

Renee: I did. I had two mediation sessions. We split the cost for the mediator, but I also had my lawyer there for me, so it cost me a lot. The actual mediation was in separate rooms, because of my anxiety about being near him. The mediator went back and forth to each room. We had two sessions that were each two hours. Those two days were expensive, but it would have saved legal fees later if it worked.

Stephanie: It didn't work?

Renee: Unfortunately, no. We made a small amount of progress the first session. For the second session, my husband added a demand for half of what I inherited from my brother. Remember, when my brother died, my husband pleaded with me to try to give our marriage a second chance. I was vulnerable and let him come back. It became clear at the second mediation session that he planned it all. Right after my brother died, he wanted the reconciliation so he could try and reset the date our marriage broke up. He wanted any inheritance I got to be part of the marital estate. He is the lowest of the low. Anyway, mediation didn't work, although I know it helps some people.

Debbie: The divorce process is awful, but better than a terrible marriage.

Stephanie: Yeah, my lawyer told me, "Peace has a price."

Renee: I definitely agree with that. You shouldn't fight over everything. Figure out what you absolutely must have to live. I didn't argue about objects in the house. I wanted to clean house of him, and I didn't care if I was left sitting on crates. The further along we were in the divorce process, the stronger I felt. I was broke, but getting stronger. I had a goal, and I could see a path more clearly to reach that goal.

Pat: I've seen many women, some very wealthy, make large adjustments in their lives. But I never heard one woman say she wished she was still married to her ex once she experienced a quieter and saner life. Some women find they actually feel more in control of their money now that they don't have to support their ex's constant demands for new toys like boats, motorcycles, and expensive cars. Once the women make the adjustment to a smaller budget, they begin to feel free.

Also I want to add my two cents about mediation. I think it's a great way to manage a divorce if you're divorcing a fairly healthy man. But a relationship with a narcissist or sociopath includes an imbalance of power, so mediation probably won't work for you. When dealing with liars, cheats and creeps, it's best to get your own lawyer, and select one who's willing to be your counsel and strong advocate. You need to feel this lawyer "has your back" and will fight for you.

Reader: Divorce is hard enough, and not knowing the outcome makes it even more scary.

Session Thirty

Leaving Takes Courage

Do I Need a Restraining Order?

Pat: Welcome back to the group, Sharon. We missed you. Let's go around and get an update from everyone.

Debbie: Cheater got another continuance from the judge on the motions before the court. It's driving me crazy, which is what he wants.

Renee: It never ends, does it?

Stephanie: I'm swamped by the financial statements I have to fill out. We have some sort of status conference with the judge in a few weeks.

Sharon: How did your husband react when you served him with divorce papers?

Stephanie: Like a raging lunatic, and he's still that way. I almost feel sorry for his lawyer. I'd like to come to a settlement, but he's irrational.

Sharon: What about your kids?

Stephanie: They're living with me, because their father doesn't have an extra room. I don't know if they want to be with him anyway. We don't have a custody issue because one son just turned 18 and the other is 16. They're angry and hurting, and my younger son slams doors a lot. He talks back to me and swears. I know they need counseling, but they refuse. The school counselor calls my 16 year old to his office, but he doesn't talk much. My boys blame me, of course.

Sharon: I just don't know what to do. My husband was out of town for ten days—and that was ten days of bliss. When he returned, he came to the house. My mom hadn't returned yet. He called to pick up the kids. I didn't say anything, just opened the door, made sure they had their overnight bags, and hugged them good-bye. My husband walked them to his car, then came back into the house and threw me across the kitchen. I hit my face on the counter. Then he left. I lay on the floor, stunned, with a bloody lip.

Debbie: Oh, no. What did you do?

Stephanie: I tried to take a selfie to show the lip, but it wasn't a good picture. The puffiness is gone now.

Renee: Did you call your lawyer about getting a restraining order?

Sharon: Yeah, but it will probably turn out the same as last time. The judge will just tell him to behave.

Debbie: Are you safe now?

Sharon: My mom came back today. It makes me feel safer, and she can babysit while I come here. I parked right in front of the door tonight. I want someone to walk me out, too. This is an awful way to live. I'm exhausted trying to be as normal as possible for my children.

Pat: Sharon, please promise me you'll go to the police and file a report on what happened the other night. You need to call the police for domestic violence. You must get these abusive outbursts on record. Going to court for a restraining order is difficult, but talk to your lawyer and try again.

Filing for a divorce is the next big decision, and only you can decide whether and when.

Renee: I used to tell myself I could leave no stone unturned to save my marriage. Then, I ran out of stones.

Sharon: I know with every cell in my body that if I file for divorce and custody of the kids, he will try to hurt me. He'll go wild. He told me so. He told me he married me for life.

Pat: That's why it's so important to file a complaint with the police. If you can't get a restraining order, at least try for a no trespassing order. He wants you to think you CANNOT divorce him. That's how he wants you to feel. What do you want?

Reader: I hope Sharon gets that restraining order. Her husband sounds like a lunatic and I'm afraid for her. I can only imagine how she feels.

Session Thirty-One

Practicing Forgiveness of Self

Pat: How's everyone doing today?

Stephanie: Well, my status conference is finally over, but then we scheduled something called a four way conference, when both people and their attorneys try and reach a settlement, or at least settle some issues. Then I think we set a court date. My case has a lot of issues and the judge said, "See what you can do." My attorney tells me the judges all want divorcing spouses to come to a settlement, so the courts only have to approve the arrangement and grant the divorce. My lawyer also said I can't afford to go through a trial.

I feel awful about all the details, the drama, and the money I don't have. I feel cornered. Do I give up on the issues and settle fast, or keep negotiating and possibly face an expensive trial? My parents are willing to help with money, but they aren't wealthy. My husband has a good paying job and his family owns a construction company, so they have a lot of bucks. This puts me at a major disadvantage.

Debbie: I'm glad you have faith in your lawyer. I wasn't happy with my attorney.

Renee: I had a good lawyer, fortunately, and she told me she would prepare for trial, but at the same time work toward an out of court settlement. I had a dollar amount I needed to live on, and there were a few ways to get there. Meanwhile my ex went through three lawyers, so you can imagine what a beast he was as a client. We settled the day before the trial, on a Sunday. My lawyer worked all day Sunday and I was at her office most of the day. I was a pool of tears, hurt, and pain. She had to deal with me and get a deal I could live with. She deserves a medal. My two sisters came to town and went with me to attend the court proceedings. We thought it would be a trial, but instead we just submitted the settlement. The judge granted me a divorce right then and there on cruel and abusive treatment, subject to the decree nisi.

Stephanie: What's that?

Renee: I learned that a decree nisi is a ninety day period before the divorce becomes final. After court, my sisters counted the ninety days on a calendar. My divorce was final on the birthday of my brother who passed away. Amazing.

Stephanie: That was a sign! How did you feel?

Renee: I actually felt kind of weird. Half of me was light headed and relieved that I finally did it—I actually divorced the monster. But I also felt scared and uncertain about the future. It's hard to explain. I didn't think I could safely drive home that day, so good thing my sisters were there. They took me to a store to buy a pot of flowers to place on my porch. That was nice, and they fixed dinner for me at the house. But they had to leave the next day and I was alone with my thoughts and my daughter.

Pat: What were your thoughts?

Renee: I was happy to finish the awful divorce, but I also felt empty. I was 55 years old, my children had also suffered through the ordeal, and I worried about the future. Plus, I felt scared of my ex. All this was on me.

Pat: Why do you say that?

Renee: I know I've talked with you about this in therapy, but I keep going back to the basic fact that I chose this man to be my husband and the father of my children. And I was the one who apparently allowed him to carry on a sordid secret life by not insisting he be at home with his family. I made hundreds of accommodations.

Pat: Do you feel the same way, Debbie?

Debbie: I feel like I wasted my best years, and I feel terrible that my wonderful children have a father who's a bastard. They deserve better. I let them down.

Stephanie: That's why I didn't want to divorce. I didn't want to take the boys' father out of their life.

Sharon: I feel that way too. I almost feel like my terrible marriage is the price I have to pay for making such a bad choice for a husband.

Pat: That's how people used to think in the old days. Divorce was socially unacceptable, so many people stayed unhappily married. Women felt trapped in abusive marriages because they had no education or job skills. But you all have options. You went to college and you can work.

Also, keep in mind that your children have been witnessing abuse and violence in your homes, which isn't healthy for them. When you divorce, your husband still has the right to see the kids and be with them, so you are not taking him out of their lives. If they choose not to see him, that is their right. If he doesn't make the effort to be in their lives, that's on him, not you. Your decision is to make your home saner and safer.

Stephanie: Okay, but that's the practical stuff. What about lying in bed at night thinking you made a complete mess of your life?

Pat: You blame yourself, right? That's a common feeling, but let me remind you of some things I've said to each of you in individual therapy:

These guys are masters of manipulation.

They lie all the time.

They are selfish and they chose to undercut your marriages with drinking, womanizing, verbal abuse, physical abuse, and being tyrannical.

They are narcissistic sociopaths who do not care about their vows to you and their responsibilities to their kids. Everything is all about them and what makes them feel good.

They like breaking the rules and they don't care who gets hurt. In fact, they enjoy hurting and controlling you.

They chased women, and in Renee's case, her husband bought women.

And they are very, very good actors.

You all had every right and expectation to believe your husbands would tell you the truth, be faithful to you, love you and your children, and make the family a priority. Do not blame yourselves for their behavior. And stop blaming yourselves for not being able to see your husbands' true colors before you married. They were charming. Being charming doesn't mean they're good people. Most sociopaths have delightful personalities on the surface. Even with a few red flags, you couldn't see the future.

Please forgive yourselves! Even therapists are fooled by clients who are sociopaths and pathological liars. Apparently, Renee's husband has been deceiving his psychiatrist for years.

The best thing you all can do is look forward, and focus your energy on building a better life, which you all completely deserve.

Debbie: What a speech! You're right, but I have to consciously not think about feeling responsible.

Renee: Me too. When I think like that, I try to concentrate on how much better life is without my ex storming around the house.

Sharon: My husband still says it's all me, and sometimes I almost believe him.

Pat: Narcissistic sociopaths always blame other people. Always. This is not about you, Sharon. It's him. When you're ready, you will make a decision. Meanwhile, make sure you and the kids are as safe as possible. Keep your cell phone with you, and hopefully your mother can stay with you. At least you have him living in his own apartment.

Reader: I'm still worried about Sharon.

Now What Should I Do?

Session Thirty-Two

Separating, or Living in the House Together During a Divorce

Pat: I'm glad everyone is here tonight. I think the group is working well with two of you on the done side of divorce and two of you still in the midst of it.

Debbie: I don't feel done with it. I'm in court all the time.

Renee: I'm done with the legal stuff, but still trying to figure out how to live.

Pat: Yes, you're both right. Divorce happens on several levels. The legal process is just one.

Stephanie: Well, I have a new problem I need help with. My soon-to-be ex is now living with his brother, and that makes my sister-in-law unhappy. She wants to know if he can stay in my basement until the divorce is over. I reminded her that he threw stuff at me and choked me. She said he wouldn't dare get near me since the divorce is underway. She tells me

151

he just needs a place to sleep and I have a rec room in the basement with a couch. So she says, "Do you want your children's father living on the street? He's broke, blah,blah... "

I asked her if he put her up to this. She said absolutely not, but I'm still not sure.

Debbie: Do you have a relationship with your sister-in-law?

Stephanie: We used to be friendly, but I haven't talked with her much since the violence, maybe twice. She called to ask if I was okay and if she could help. That was nice. Her kids and mine have grown up together.

Renee: She's in a tough place between her husband and your husband.

Stephanie: What should I do, Pat?

Pat: Do not allow your husband back in your house! He was abusive to you and that will escalate, not settle down! There are times when I advise couples to have a trial separation in the house. It's a cooling off period while the couple continues with counseling. Either the issues are aired and settled or they're not. And if not, then one of them moves out of the house and the couple pursues a divorce. But, I would never recommend staying in the house together after physical violence occurs, and that's exactly the situation you're in, Stephanie.

Renee: When my husband and I first went to marriage counseling, we were told to separate in the house. I moved to an extra room we had on the third floor for about two weeks. Then he said he wanted us to get back. I was relieved, and hopeful—and obviously completely clueless.

Pat: It isn't easy to separate in or out of the house, and you may second guess yourself again and again. But Stephanie, I want you to hear again that I never advise anyone to live in the same house when violence has occurred. Your husband is an alcoholic and an abuser. Stay firm. He'll find a place to stay. He's resourceful, and he has all those drinking buddies. And his parents are wealthy –right? You need to focus on completing the divorce.

Stephanie: Yeah, he can go to his parents, or maybe he can just hole up in his favorite place, the bar!

Reader: Separating, then divorcing, then starting a new life. What have we left out?

Session Thirty-Three

Telling the Children

Pat: Each of you has children at different ages. Sharon and I spoke earlier this week about her kids and I suggested she bring her concerns to the group. Is that okay with everyone?

Debbie: Sure. This is my least favorite topic: how I hurt my kids because I married Cheater.

Renee: I agree. It's probably the most painful part of the divorce, at least for me. Sharon, your kids obviously know your husband has his own place now.

Sharon: Yes, they do. My husband is renting a house. They go there once a week and he took them on a vacation.

Renee: Without you.

Sharon: That's right.

Debbie: What did you tell them when your husband moved out?

Sharon: I told them Mommy and Daddy needed a break to solve some problems, so Daddy was going to live in a new place for a while. He would be nearby. Then I told them they'd still see him often. At the time, I made it seem temporary. That was all I could deal with right then. I'm trying to figure out what to say when I file the divorce papers. I'm pretty sure I've decided to do it this week, but telling my kids is the hardest part. How did you all tell your kids?

Stephanie: Being choked by their father and having cops at the house tipped them off that there was trouble in paradise. But, seriously, my boys are teenagers and they've lived through all the shouting and drinking. I told them straight out that I was getting a restraining order and their father was out. My oldest asked what was going to happen. At the time, I didn't know. I told my boys I needed to figure things out and would be talking to a lawyer. He then asked if we were going to be divorced and I told him I didn't know, but the violence had to stop.

Sharon: What about the younger one—he's about 16, right?

Stephanie: Yeah. He got quiet and went to his room.

Renee: And what about when you told your sons you decided to get a divorce?

Stephanie: It actually didn't seem like such a big deal to them. They saw the separation wasn't fixing anything. Their father continued bad mouthing me non-stop and he even told them I was to blame for breaking up our family. I think he scared them about how poor they were going to be. They want things to be the same at school and with their friends. They didn't really seem to care about the marriage itself, just how poor we were going to be.

Pat: That's very common, especially for teenagers. They don't want anyone to know. They want to try and carry on in their world as though nothing happened, and they're often preoccupied with having things that make them feel like they fit in. Renee, your children knew right away too?

Renee: Yes, and I mean right away. On the night of the gonorrhea bomb, my 16 year old daughter had just gone to bed in her room down the hall. She must have heard everything. I talked to her the next morning, and she looked kind of frozen sitting on the couch. I told her that her dad and I were having a big argument, and we would work something out. As for my other three other kids, I talked to them that day also. Since my youngest daughter at home overheard it all, her older brothers and sister needed to know. They all needed to know why their family blew up. The news of separating wasn't the bomb. The bomb was their father's horrible behavior.

Sharon: You told your children their father got gonorrhea from a prostitute?

Renee: You betcha. They're old enough to know the truth. I'd have put a notice in the newspaper if I thought of it. Our marriage was over and my health was at stake. I also told my older kids when I tested positive. I was proud of my oldest son. The first time he came home, he physically threw his father out the back door onto the driveway. My kids were all disgusted and hurting.

Sharon: Pat, how do I tell my kids when I file for divorce? They're so little. How can I get a divorce if I have to fight for custody?

Pat: We'll talk about custody soon. Kids don't choose their parents, and they can feel lost, powerless, worried, and responsible. Your job is to assure them you're there and your love for them is steady. You also need to reassure them they didn't cause the divorce. For now, you have four basic and essential things to tell your kids. Repeat these often and with love:

1) Mom and Dad don't love each other the way two people need to love to stay married.

2) You didn't cause the divorce.

3) I will try to keep things the same if I can—same schools, same neighborhood, and hopefully the same house, at least for a while.

4) I love you, and that will never change.

Reader: Divorce is definitely not just between the husband and wife. Everything turns upside down. I would need a good lawyer to help me get through a divorce. How do you get the right lawyer to help?

Session Thirty-Four

Divorce: Just Do It, But With the Right Attorney

Pat: Hi everybody. Sharon, let's start with you.

Sharon: I've got big news: I filed for a divorce.

Pat: Wow, that was fast. Can you tell us how you got to your decision?

Sharon: I think I was sick of feeling like a caged bird. And when the judge wouldn't protect me with a restraining order, I began to think I had to protect myself by getting out. So I guess the judge helped me by telling my husband to behave himself. I realized no one understands what a sick psycho he is. You all know I haven't been happy for a long time with my husband's controlling behavior. And it's been getting much worse over the last year or so, including the time when he threw me against the wall in the garage. That's when I called the police. He has also locked me out of the house, and even pushed me out of a moving car. He has forced me to have sex, so he raped me. He moved out when I went to court for the restraining order, even though I didn't get it (which I still can't believe). The judge warned him to behave himself—and that was supposed to protect me?

Pat: It's important to call the police every time violence occurs, so they have a record, regardless of what ultimately happens in court.

Sharon: Right. So he rented a house about a mile away and he's been awful since then. He drives around the block a lot, and I think he parks at the end of the street at night. He texts me about how I can't win. He has the kids on Saturday nights. This past Sunday, my kids were agitated when he dropped them off at the end of the driveway. My daughter told me: "Daddy hates you." His text to me before he drove away was: "You'll regret this."

It seems like he knows when I meet with my lawyer. It's creepy. Nothing between us is better with the separation. In fact, everything is worse. I can't imagine myself living with him ever again, so I had to file for divorce. At this point, I feel I have no choice.

Pat: You're better off without him. That is precisely the realization that comes with a separation.

Debbie: Are you scared?

Sharon: Yes, very. I'm worn out by fear.

Renee: Do you like your attorney?

Sharon: What do you mean?

Renee: A good lawyer will take some of the burden of negotiating away from you and block your husband from contacting you directly. Is she representing you competently?

Sharon: I think so. I've never been divorced before, so I have nothing to compare it to. A friend recommended her.

Renee: Find out as much as you can about the lawyer. Recommendations from people you trust are important, and it's good if your friend was satisfied with this lawyer. I know this lawyer, too. She knows the law, but divorce situations are so intensely personal, you want to have good rapport with her. I spoke with two other lawyers before I selected one. You need to know that she'll answer your questions. Is she keeping you informed?

Sharon: I think so.

Debbie: It's important to have a lawyer who listens to you and answers your questions. She needs to explain the pros and cons of your options and then give her recommendations.

Sharon: We have a pretty good rapport. I had to give her a big retainer, so she'd better answer my questions. She sends me a lot of stuff by email.

Debbie: What is the basis for the divorce?

Sharon: Irreconcilable differences. Talk about a massive understatement!

Debbie: Irreconcilable differences is the most common reason for divorce in this state. Most divorces end with a settlement which is all about the details of your finances, so it's important that your lawyer knows how much money you need to live on.

Sharon: I never thought I'd ever get a divorce.

Debbie: None of us did. That's why we waited and waited.

Sharon: My kids are little, remember. My lawyer said that divorce and custody are separate.

Debbie: Technically, yes, but your kids and your assets are all part of the whole process of divorcing from your husband.

Pat: Who else does Sharon need to help her get through the divorce?

Renee: An accountant and a financial advisor. Sometimes that's the same person, and sometimes two different people. Have you filled out the court forms stating your income and expenses?

Sharon: Yes, it was hard. He handles the money.

Pat: It's common for one spouse to be in charge of the money. You're smart, Sharon. You can handle money matters going forward—right?

Sharon: Absolutely yes. I took care of myself before I got married.

Pat: That's great.

Debbie: If you ever need help planning, I have a financial advisor you might like.

Sharon: Thanks.

Debbie: And make sure you understand what's going on. If you don't get what your lawyer is talking about, ask her to explain. This is what they do every day, and you aren't expected to know it.

Stephanie: I feel kind of dumb when I ask my lawyer questions. I sometimes have to ask the same thing again and again, because I just don't get it.

Renee: That's okay. You're not a lawyer or an accountant, but it's a good idea to write down your questions and take notes on the answers. I had to write everything down because I couldn't remember anything—and I know accounting!

Debbie: I made different piles of papers to stay organized. I had the business and the house, so I had business loans, a house mortgage, life insurance, health expenses and insurance, taxes, and a pile for each of the kids.

Stephanie: I have one big pile on a table in my room.

Debbie: You'll help yourself and your lawyer if you break it down into categories that make sense to you. Go get some expandable file folders, or at least make separate piles in your bedroom. With your kids at home, I wouldn't leave any papers around.

Renee: Listen to your lawyer and follow her advice. And stay in some sort of therapy, because the emotional stuff goes on long after the divorce.

Pat: Stress makes it hard to understand new things and keep things organized. These tips sound like good advice.

Reader: You have to get organized in order to get divorced? It sounds like you have to get your house in order just to tear it apart.

Session Thirty-Five

Backsliding

Pat: Let's start tonight by checking in with everyone.

Debbie: I have another meeting with my new lawyer to get ready to file a third contempt motion. Cheater owes me money.

Stephanie: You have a new lawyer?

Debbie: Yes, to represent me on a new lawsuit, because Cheater only pays me when we're about to go to court. I feel like this will never end.

Renee: I'm okay, but I am worried about my kids.

Pat: Sharon, you look tired.

Sharon: I am beyond tired. I'm flat out exhausted and I'm buried in details. All I want is to be a good mom to my kids. I want this whole thing to be over as soon as possible.

Stephanie: I've been sleep deprived for about a year. It's exhausting to make so many huge life decisions and keep track of all the details. I stare at the ceiling and toss and turn all night. Then I have to go to work and be cheerful. After that, I have to deal with my teenagers who are being difficult. I couldn't wait to have my divorce done. But don't be too eager to settle.

Sharon: What do you mean?

Stephanie: Well... drum roll please. I have a settlement.

Pat: That's great. I wondered why you were smiling there with your head down. I knew something was up.

Stephanie: It's good news, but also maybe not so good. The day before we were supposed to go to court, my lawyer kept telling me almost any settlement we could make that day would be better than a settlement made by a judge. She also kept reminding me I couldn't afford her fees to go to trial. So I was determined we would get a settlement by 5 o'clock. I knew the bare minimum for alimony and child support I needed, and I got that. But now I realize that I shouldn't have given up on insurance and taxes. My lawyer often told me that peace has a price, so make sure to know what is absolutely essential and what to let go. I figured I'd be selling or refinancing the house in a few months, so I could just drop my insurance. Now, I feel I caved in on insurance issues. I have to borrow more money from my parents to pay the current premium on my house insurance and my car insurance, and real estate taxes weren't part of the settlement at all. I have no money at all for my kids.

Pat: So what is your advice for Sharon?

Stephanie: Don't rush through the details like I did! Make sure you think about every expense individually. I agreed to be responsible for all those expenses that go with the divided asset—which is something I did just to get it over with. Now I have a house, but with a part time job I can't pay the insurance or taxes. I probably won't be able to pay the heating bill this winter. I'm panicking.

Pat: It's common for women in the midst of a separation and divorce process to get tired and stressed. They want it to end more than anything else. Sometimes they "backslide" just to get it done, but later they regret not sticking to the original demands. Hang in there, Sharon, and get what you need from your divorce to make a comfortable life for yourself and your kids. Make sure you're also taking care of yourself now—eating and getting enough sleep. You need to be strong and alert.

Stephanie: Does this backsliding thing happen to men? It doesn't seem so.

Pat: You're right that it doesn't seem to. Men are often more into fighting. In each of your cases your husbands used negotiations and the whole divorce process to torment and punish you. They need to "win" the divorce and crush you, even though divorce shouldn't be a game to win or lose.

Sharon: I definitely want this to end. I don't think I can do this. There are too many details.

Pat: It seems un-doable at first. But with the help of your attorney and the support of this group, you can manage. Hang in there, Sharon! Online, or from your attorney, you can get a worksheet with lists of things to do during a divorce. Your accountant or financial advisor can also give you a to-do list. You can do this, Sharon!

Stephanie: Why do women seem to cave in more often? Are we weak or something?

Pat: Exhaustion, feeling overwhelmed by details, being uncertain of the future, and sometimes even nostalgia for the best days with your husbands. You all tried to fix your marriages and now you're trying to fix things quickly through the divorce process. You each absorbed a lot—and it may seem easier to concede on issues. As I said, backsliding is common. Some women even stop the divorce process completely.

Renee: I didn't backslide, but I wish my ex would slide far away. Like down into a sink hole to the center of the earth.

Pat: Renee, we know how you're feeling, but you got the divorce and he's out of your life.

Sharon: I don't get why backsliding is a worry. What's wrong with wanting it to be over? Maybe an easy settlement will make my husband calm down.

Pat: I don't want you to make a hasty settlement just to get it over with. That is the opposite extreme of arguing over every dish in the house. With your lawyer, figure out what you need and stay firm on those issues. As for the small stuff—I agree it's good to let go and not argue just to fight. But, be aware that sometimes the lawyers are sick of the case and want to get it over. You need to be sure you aren't settling too soon.

Stephanie: You can do this, Sharon. I did, and you can too.

Sharon: Thanks, Stephanie. Thanks to everyone. I just hope I'm not found wandering the streets in my bathrobe some night in the near future.

Pat: I know that won't happen. Keep your eye on the goal of getting out of an unhealthy marriage and you will have a better life for you and your kids.

Reader: Stay focused, Sharon, and be strong!

Session Thirty-Six

Practical Tips about Contact

(Phone, Email, and Social Media)

Pat: I realize I've given you many tips during our meetings. Maybe it's worthwhile to compile a list for Sharon and other women in the process of divorce. Let's start with collective wisdom about contact with your exes during and after the divorce:

- Block your cell phone, home phone, and email setting from your ex and any other people you don't want to hear from. If you need help with the tech part, go to the online help sites, visit the store where you purchased your cell phone, call a helpline, or ask a friend.

- Defriend him and his family on Facebook.

- Ask your friends and others in your family to defriend him, or at least ask them not to post any information about you.

- Change your phone number. If you're getting unwanted calls, then request an unlisted number.

- Delete his name from your cell phone contacts or substitute "Children's Father" if you decide to allow him to call and text you.

- There are many Apps for people in fear of domestic abuse. Some allow you to call for help with disguised names and emergency exit buttons. Others alert you to when your domestic abuser is near.

- Apps like OurFamilyWizard give subscribers joint custody tools, including child custody calendars, shared visitation schedules, secure messaging, family information storage (immunizations and important contacts), and shared expense payments.

- If you're the one paying for your children's phones, they may want to block him on their phones if he's being abusive. If he wants to phone them, he can pay for phones and phone service for them. Sometimes, details about the phones for the kids are part of the custody or settlement agreement.

- Be careful of your own posts and emails, because they may be subject to discovery by the other side in a contested divorce or custody battle.

- Keep all voicemails, texts, and emails from your husband.

- Keep voicemail, texts, and emails your kids show you from their father if the messages are alarming.

- Tell your family and your kids not to answer his questions about you or give details about your life. Tell them to say "I'm not going to talk about her at all." Eventually, he will stop trying to get information about you from others.

- Use your lawyer to communicate with him. Don't talk, text, or email him directly.

Reader: These tips should be helpful before, during, and after a divorce.

Session Thirty-Seven

Dividing Your Life

Pat: Hi, everyone. Good to see you all. Sharon, I think you have some news?

Sharon: Yes. I just got a divorce

Debbie: What? How did it happen so fast?

Renee: Oh, my gosh! That's great!

Stephanie: How did you get an accelerated divorce? And congratulations!

Debbie and Renee: Congratulations!

Pat: Amazing, Sharon. Tell us how this happened so quickly.

Debbie: Yeah, my divorce took years.

Renee: Mine too.

Sharon: I was afraid my divorce would take years, but the attorneys negotiated like crazy during the past week and we reached an agreement on alimony, child support, the house, the cars, income taxes for this year, health insurance, and some investments. I think both lawyers knew they had to get things done during a brief window of opportunity when my husband was in a reasonable mood. His own lawyer seemed sick of him. I was blown away when my attorney told me he agreed to our core requests. She recommended I grab it before he had a chance to become petty and monstrous again. I trust my attorney, so I went with the deal.

Renee: Do you have a restraining order as part of the agreement?

Sharon: No, I don't think so. I get the house as soon as a deed is prepared, and he'd better sign it. I'm just worried because things happened so fast there might be problems later on.

Renee: He didn't sign a deed when he signed the settlement agreement?

Sharon: No, my lawyer is preparing it now. It all happened fast.

Stephanie: If you don't have a restraining order, you can go to the police department and file a no trespass order.

Sharon: Do I have to wait for the deed from him?

Debbie: I don't think you need it. Just take the settlement agreement and show the section giving you the house. A no trespass order will at least keep him away from your home, because if he ignores it and goes there, he can be arrested for trespassing. That's faster than filing a contempt order in court.

Sharon: I called a security company to install video cameras. But he still has to come into the house to get the furniture and other stuff he wants.

Renee: What do you mean? Didn't you divide the contents of the house already?

Sharon: No, not really. And he said "You better not have removed anything, because I'll know."

Pat: It sounds like the lawyers knew they had a basic deal he was willing to sign and they went for it. You said he's been difficult to deal with, right?

Sharon: Yes, horrible. He lost his temper a lot, but he must have been in a good mood that day to sign a settlement. My lawyer says dividing the contents of the house will happen in the next thirty days and is supposed to be a good faith equal division of the contents of the home. It could be a circus if he becomes his normal self. I overheard the lawyers saying dividing the house contents will be a "shit show." Weird, huh?

Renee: I think your lawyers are right about that. Usually it's best if the settlement takes care of everything, but it sounds like your attorney got what she could from him.

Sharon: Yes. Now I dread him coming into the house and picking over things.

Pat: I recommend you not be there when he comes over. Have your attorney there and a representative for you.

Sharon: How can I not be there?

Pat: You can make a list of things you want in the house, and have your attorney there to handle it for you. He will try to use the division of the things in the house to hurt you more. Do not be there.

Sharon: But I don't want him in the house alone.

Pat: How did you others handle this?

Debbie: Cheater didn't take anything. He eventually bought a house and furnished it himself. He got the restaurant and everything in it.

Stephanie: My ex took a lot of stuff over the first months he was out of the house. My boys would also take things to him that he asked for. When we signed the settlement papers he listed tools that were in the basement and garage. I had no problem about that, except the lawn mower. He wanted the lawn mower even though he doesn't have a lawn. Can you believe that? Anyway, we scheduled a time for him to come over and take everything out of the garage, but I stayed away. He came over with his buddy and I had my father and a friend watch the house. My ex doesn't want to mess with my father.

Pat: Stephanie, your ex wanted the lawn mower as a dig at you. Some mundane things like a lawn mower are infused with meaning. Without it, he knew you'd need to hand mow your lawn or spend money to replace the mower. He wants you to think about him whenever you mow your lawn.

I have clients that argue at length over a piece of furniture or equipment, but it's not about the item itself—it's about the emotion connected to it.

Renee: Sharon, do you have expensive stuff and family heirlooms?

Sharon: Yes. We bought good furniture, paintings, place settings, and lots of stuff. We received nice wedding gifts, too. My mom gave me some of the family silver for our wedding and my birthdays since then.

Renee: I'll tell you what I did. I gathered all the stuff in the house that was his in any way, shape, or form and put it in the front hallway or on the porch. When he moved out of the house two years earlier, he took all his clothes and he moved some furniture to a friend's garage. But I sorted out every remaining dish, tablecloth, lamp, table, painting, book, album and CD—everything that was connected to him or his family, and it went into boxes in the front hallway. I wanted him to take it all away. If he left anything, I would have donated it to Goodwill. My daughter and I were out of the house during the time he agreed to come, and my brother-in-law and sister were there to make sure he didn't walk around the whole house or take anything else. My brother-in- law could have reached me by cell phone if anything came up. The garage was a separate issue though.

Sharon: What do you mean?

Renee: He had an old car sitting in our driveway for at least 25 years. As long as it was there, he didn't have to rent garage space somewhere. So this old car, his bikes, and all his tools were still there. My lawyer arranged for a police officer to be at my house on a specified day so my ex could take the car and all the remaining stuff in the garage. I stayed away during this time. My lawyer told me to make a receipt for it all, and I gave the receipt to the policeman, who had my ex sign it.

Sharon: What if my husband takes what doesn't belong to him? I expect him to try.

Debbie: You can make a list of items you claim and give the list to your lawyer. Ask if you can remove the items or just store them in a locked closet. I think you should do what Renee did and hire a police officer. Also have a family member or a friend there, preferably a male. Be available by cell phone only if necessary.

Sharon: He already told me I'd better not lock anything or remove anything before he gets there.

Stephanie: When did he say that?

Sharon: He said it to me after the hearing with the judge when the lawyers gave her the settlement and she granted the divorce.

Pat: He's such a creep! Don't talk to him at all. Let your lawyer handle this. If the lawyers think it will be a big problem, let them be the ones in the line of fire!

Sharon: You should know that before the hearing he came up to me to ask if I would stop everything. I told him to leave me alone.

Debbie: Your lawyer shouldn't have let him to talk to you.

Sharon: I was a few minutes early and as soon as I turned the corner, he jumped up from where he was sitting and rushed over to me.

Pat: He continues trying to manipulate you, and when he can't, he turns angry and abusive. If you treasure certain items, let the lawyers know he can't have them.

Expect him to take stuff he thinks will make you angry. If they are items you purchased together as a couple, know the value of them so you can make sure what he takes and leaves is equal in value. And, if at all possible, detach your emotions from the items in your house. Protect what you can with your lawyer, but for everything else—let it go with him. He wants to hurt you and he'd love to fight with you over anything, down to the smallest teacup. Let things go and loosen the emotional rope so if he yanks it, you don't feel it.

Renee: Just make sure that whatever he claims is his goes with him that day, because there should not be another time.

Sharon: Okay. That's good advice.

Renee: After my ex took everything out of the hallway, I came home and sat in a chair, feeling numb. My sister rearranged the remaining furniture and paintings that night. My house already looked less cluttered, all his stuff was gone, and it was all fine. It was more than fine. I felt lighter. It was liberating.

Reader: This sounds like spring cleaning your life. But what about the kids?

Session Thirty-Eight

Custody Battles, Guardian Ad Litem Reports, and Supervised Visits

Pat: What about custody? For three of you, the children were older when you got a divorce so custody wasn't an issue. But Sharon has a five and seven year old, and she's concerned about custody.

Sharon: I'm worried about my kids. I told them about the divorce and that I loved them. I told them the four things on the list you gave me, Pat. I told them they would be going to their father's on Saturday. Both kids started crying. They don't want to go. My daughter said she didn't think she'd have to go to his house anymore once we got a divorce. Their attitudes really surprised me.

Pat: Children often jump to conclusions. Keep assuring them of your love and they have their home with you. As much as you can, explain to them how often they'll see their Dad. Sharon has an added complication—a 51A was filed by the school.

Stephanie: What's that?

Pat: A 51A is the notification by a mandated reporter to the Department of Children and Family Services that abuse or neglect is suspected. Sharon's children see a counselor at school and a psychologist, and both were concerned enough to file a 51A on their father for neglect and physical abuse and sexual abuse.

Stephanie: Oh, no. That's horrible. What is a mandated reporter?

Pat: In our state, a pediatrician, a school nurse, a teacher, and a counselor. I am a mandated reporter. If we suspect abuse or neglect of a child in our care, we file a notice with the state to request an investigation.

Stephanie: What do you think?

Sharon: I think my ex-husband neglected my kids when he left them alone in a hotel room where he went during their last vacation. He has also thrown my kids around and shoved them. And, recently my kids told the counselor their father takes their cell phones when they go to his house. My son also told us his dad sleeps with him, holding him, and gives them full-body wrap around hugs. The psychologist says it's inappropriate touching, and he thinks the kids should only have supervised visitation with him. When she spoke with my son, the school counselor was concerned about how scared he sounded, so she felt she had to file a 51A, too.

Renee: How does supervised visitation work?

Pat: This is something ordered by a judge. Several locations in this area have trained social workers who monitor visits from a parent with a child. The child is never left alone. You have to sign up for the time. This is the only safe way in many cases.

Sharon: I want full custody and full visitation.

Pat: There are two types of custody: physical and legal. Physical custody refers to where the children live most of the time. Some divorced parents have shared or joint physical custody where each parent has the children 50% of the time. Others have sole physical custody where one parent has the children most of the time and the other parent only has visitation rights. Typically a visitation schedule would be every other weekend and maybe a night or two during the week for a two or three hour dinner visit. If there's any concern about a child's safety, that calls for supervised visits in a licensed supervised center.

Legal custody is usually shared by both parents and refers to decisions about the children, such as where they go to school, what church they attend, and medical decisions. When there are serious concerns about a person's ability to parent, the other parent gets sole legal custody.

Sharon, what has happened with the 51A filed on your husband?

Sharon: A woman from the Department of Child and Family Services interviewed me and also spoke with both children. I understand she also plans to interview the psychologist and school counselor.

Another person called a guardian ad litem is involved from the courts, and she's collecting information for the custody hearing. She toured my house a few days ago and I assume she interviewed my ex and visited the house he's renting. My ex-husband asked for alternating weekends, two vacations during the school year, and a month each summer. I don't get how he thinks he can have joint physical custody if a 51A was filed. He also wants joint legal custody, which would keep him involved in every school conference and every medical appointment. I feel like I'm not even divorced.

Pat: Filing a 51A is just a start and what mandated reporters have to do. Now it's up to the Department of Child and Family Services to see if the complaints are substantiated. A lot of filings are not substantiated, so your husband still may be able to get visitation rights to the children. I cannot stress this enough: keep your children in counseling at school and with a private psychologist. If anything happens to them, they already have a mandated reporter who will help.

Stephanie: Another thing: the judge will probably order you to take parenting classes for divorced parents.

Sharon: What was that like? I'm a good parent.

Stephanie: I think the person who taught the parenting class I attended was a social worker. She explained how not to place the kids in the middle of arguments—stuff like that. I went and listened to what they had to say, but I don't think my ex went. Or if he did go, he certainly didn't listen. I also don't think these teachers understand about narcissistic, sociopathic ex-husbands.

177

Pat: Parenting classes have become pretty standard for divorced parents with kids. I agree that most of these classes assume you can work cooperatively with your exes, which isn't the case when you're dealing with sociopaths.

I always recommend that kids go to counselors at school or outside of school to talk over their feelings before, during, and after the divorce. If there is neglect or abuse of any kind, we want the kids to be able to tell a trusted adult in addition to their mother.

Sharon, are you worried about this weekend?

Sharon: I am very worried about this weekend and the vacation next month. My kids don't want to go with him at all, and the guardian ad litem hasn't written her report yet so the Department of Child and Family Services has done nothing.

Pat: Ask the worker from DCF to tell you what the status is. Once the Department investigates and the guardian ad litem writes her report to the judge, and if they agree with the counselor, then hopefully, the judge will order only supervised visitation.

Sharon: I hope so, and I wish they'd hurry. My kids both say they have stomach aches now. Saturday will be awful.

Pat: Update your pediatrician about the divorce and your suspicions. The pediatrician is also a mandated reporter and should be on the lookout for signs of abuse and neglect. Also let the school nurse know.

Reader: The divorce may be over, but problems with custody and visitations with the children are just beginning.

Note:
Rules surrounding notification of abuse and neglect and types of custody may vary from state to state.

Fallout after Divorce

Session Thirty-Nine

How to Limit Contact with an Ex, Even with Children

Pat: All four of you are divorced ladies now. How do you feel?

Debbie: It's not over for me. I still have a lawsuit going for money Cheater owes me.

Renee: For me, it's over and it's not over. I feel different things at different times. I feel good when I look forward, but there are things I don't do because I don't want to see my ex.

Stephanie: I hear about my ex from my boys all the time, and I see him at soccer and baseball games at least once a week.

Renee: I would hate that. How do you handle it?

Stephanie: I sit with people I know, and Pat said don't go to the parking lot alone. I can't block him from my cell phone, because we have to coordinate who'll be picking up the kids from practice.

Pat: Is there any reason for your ex to talk to you about anything other than the kids?

Stephanie: Not as long as he sends the checks on time, like he's supposed to.

Pat: Do you want to talk to him directly?

Stephanie: Hell, no.

Pat: All right then! Look into an APP like FamilyWizard that shows activities on a calendar and which parent is responsible for what. Sharon, do you use it?

Sharon: I'm using it for basic scheduling. The weekends he has the kids are on it and everything else is mine. But I don't want him to have custody at all.

Pat: Any news on the DCF report?

Sharon: No.

Pat: Your children still have their counselors. Keep those lines of communication open. And since you now have Family Wizard, have you blocked him from your cell phone and email?

Sharon: Yes, but I was surprised to see him at a neighbor's open house.

Renee: What happened?

Sharon: I didn't even know how he knew about the party or why he was there. My friend was surprised, too. She pulled me aside when I arrived and told me he was there. I turned around and left.

Pat: Why?

Sharon: I don't want to see him. I'm sure he came just to torment me, and I didn't want my friend to feel any tension with both of us there.

Pat: Was he alone or with a girlfriend?

Sharon: I think he was alone, but I don't know.

Pat: How did you feel?

Sharon: I was shaking. I went to my car and drove home shaking.

Debbie: You poor thing. I'm sure your ex was there just to be a jerk.

Sharon: No doubt about that. I feel awful that my friend had to deal with him and our divorce.

Pat: Remember, narcissists think only about themselves and sociopaths don't even register emotion; they just think about manipulation and harming you.

Renee: I would do exactly the same thing, Sharon. I used to go to the symphony, but not anymore. Pat, I know you think I should do whatever I want and go wherever I want to go without thinking about my ex, but it's not so easy. I don't want to buy tickets to a concert, see him there, and have to leave.

Pat: You don't have to leave, but I get that he still creeps you out and makes you feel uncomfortable.

Renee: I wouldn't be able to enjoy the concert if he was there, so I would leave.

Pat: I do understand that going places isn't easy when you fear your ex will be there. I just hate to think you can't enjoy doing things you love because the liar, cheat and creep is there. I would love if all of you could go out as you want, but don't go out alone. Take someone to support you.

These men should not be able to fence you in. Your ex has remarried Renee. I think he's moved on.

Renee: This is one of the few times I disagree with you, Pat. My ex is not stable. I know he's capable of anything at any time. I thought he was happily married to me—and yet he bought and exploited hundreds of women. Being married didn't block his bad behavior, so I fear being divorced and re-married won't keep him in check. He's conniving, secretive, and awful.

Pat: I understand. I guess I just want you to be free of him.

Renee: I want to be rid of him.

Pat: I would like you to feel free in your mind from him, even if he's in the same room. But I know that's difficult, if not impossible, when you've been abused by someone.

Renee: I blocked him from my phones and emails, and I don't go where I think I'll see him. I do work on feeling free of him and his abuse. My decision not to go to a concert is a small price to pay for not seeing his awful face. I really don't want to ever see him again and I don't want to hear about him either.

Pat: Okay. Maybe we all experience freedom in different ways. First and foremost you need to feel safe and do what's comfortable for you.

Renee: I feel as soon as I let my guard down, he'll do something to me.

Debbie: Do you have friends in common?

Renee: No, none. And some of his relatives don't want anything to do with him either.

Sharon: I was surprised my ex came to the open house. I have to think about where I go.

Pat: Just try to not go out to an event alone. Always be with a supportive friend or two.

Sharon: That's impossible. I'm a single woman now.

Pat: Okay, but whenever possible, go with a friend or friends. I think he'll eventually tire of showing up to bother you.

Debbie: I see my ex from time to time, and I see stuff about him on Facebook.

Pat: You still follow him on Facebook?

Debbie: Yes. Knowledge is power.

Renee: You have a different strategy than me. I don't want to know anything about my ex at all.

Pat: You two are examples of a common problem: Renee is still avoiding her ex and Debbie, you still follow your ex. Neither of you has totally disengaged.

Renee: Not until I'm far away, or he dies, will I feel safe.

Sharon: Same for me. But I know someone who has a cordial relationship with her ex-husband.

Pat: Sometimes that happens, and it's nice when it does. But your husbands are narcissists and abusive, so you need to stay away from them. However, distance can be actual miles as well as psychic distance. Even if he lives nearby as all your ex-husbands do, you can separate your emotional connections. Sharon, what if your ex gets a girlfriend or remarries? How will you feel?

Sharon: I certainly won't be jealous, if that's what you're asking. Any woman he dates will just be his next victim. In fact, I hope he meets someone and relocates far away. As you once told us, the next woman can be a good distraction.

Renee: I also feel no jealousy at all. I don't even know his new wife's name. It just doesn't matter at all. He's a misogynist, so he always needs a woman to control or abuse.

Stephanie: I will always live with my ex around town. His whole family lives here and I see him at school events.

Sharon: You have no custody issues, right?

Stephanie: Right. My sons see their father when and if they want to. They call him when they need a ride or money—and if they want to party on the weekends. He just lets them hang out and drink even though they're underage. He is such a poor father. I'd like to move closer to my parents, and I may do that after my youngest son graduates from high school.

Sharon: I think my husband will stay in the area, try to get custody of the kids, and continue trying to wreck my life.

Pat: Now that you have the surveillance cameras and alarm system, do you feel safer in your home, Sharon? I hope so. You used to belong to a country club; do you still go there with the boys?

Sharon: No way. I don't set foot in that club anymore. Instead, I play tennis with my best friend at her club or play tennis and swim at the community courts and pool. If my husband wants to take the kids to the country club he can, and he might just do that to show them off. Like, "Look at me, I'm father of the year!" He disgusts me! Yet, I'll have to deal with him for years because my kids are young. I worry about them every minute they're with him.

Pat: We'll work on that more in individual therapy. But I keep repeating that you should all pay attention to the present and the future, take care of yourselves and your kids, and fill your lives with as many positive people and activities as possible. Just going for a walk with a friend is good for body and soul. Keep working on detaching from these awful men. Remember, you can work on how to create emotional distance from them.

Sharon: Detaching is hard when I still have to deal with my ex around my small children almost every day.

Stephanie: Yes, it's very hard, even when the children are teenagers, like in my case.

Pat: Parenting kids after a divorce is always a challenge, even when the parents can set aside their emotions and focus on what's best for the kids.

Stephanie: Yeah, in the parenting class, the teacher kept reminding us that the kids didn't do anything wrong, yet they can be hurt a lot when parents argue. But my ex is abusive to me. I'm going to tell him to shut up whenever he calls me names.

Pat: Parenting classes ordered by the court don't usually consider the fact that one of the parents may be an abuser and a sociopath. For your own safety, none of you will be able to have nice chats about your kids' report cards with your exes. Use the scheduling apps to post visits, games, events, and who needs to pick up or drop off.

Sharon, what's going on with your custody issue?

Sharon: The guardian ad litem gave the judge a report that she had concerns about neglect and the appropriateness of touching. So the judge ordered my ex to attend the parenting class and get individual counseling. Also, a designated person will pop in at unannounced times when he has the kids. The Department of Child and Family Services report said the abuse was unsubstantiated and closed the case. They recommended the boys stay in therapy.

Debbie: Not supervised visits?

Sharon: No. This judge seems incapable of seeing through my ex. His lawyer is so slick. He told the judge how much stress his client has been under and how he didn't even want the divorce and blah, blah, blah. The judge accepted it all.

Renee: So what's the result?

Sharon: I have the kids during the week and he'll have them every other weekend, during school vacation weeks, and for one month in the summer. I'm freaking out about it. My kids are also freaking out.

Pat: They need to continue to see the counselor. I think the court made a mistake in your case, Sharon. Your young children should have supervised visits. That's why they will continue needing a psychologist they can talk to about anything scary or inappropriate that happens when they're with their father.

Sharon: Absolutely. But I feel like I can't protect them. They're upset before and after seeing their father.

Pat: Ask their counselor to explain to them about impermissible touching. I'm sure he's already done that. Your kids will need to learn all about boundaries. Tell them to report anything at all that worries them to the counselor, and to you of course. The counselor will file another 51A if the need arises.

Sharon: My kids shouldn't have to deal with this.

Reader: How do you ever heal if you have children with a man you're divorced from? Those poor kids. If only they had a better, healthier father.

Session Forty

Guilt: Why Is He My Children's Father?

Pat: We talked last time about difficult topics that affect our children. Sharon, you're crying. Why?

Sharon: My kids were with my ex overnight on Saturday, and my son said his father still does the Johnny Hug, which he hates.

Stephanie: What is that?

Sharon: My husband wraps himself around Johnny's body and wiggles. What he's doing is rubbing his penis against my son.

Stephanie: That's disgusting.

Sharon: Yes it is. And the judge allows this to go on.

Pat: When do the kids see their counselor?

Sharon: Tomorrow. They were so upset when they got out of his car and walked into the house.

Debbie: Do you drive your kids to his house for the visit and pick them up?

Sharon: No, my mom drives them over and retrieves them. She's a saint, but she's also upset when she returns because her grandchildren are telling her they don't want to go to their father's house. My kids are acting out at home now. Johnny stormed past me into his room and slammed the door.

Pat: That's another sign of the stress he's under. Give the kids time to decompress when they first come home. Tell them it's their coming back home time. But the next day, be clear and comforting about the rules when they're back at home, such as no back talk or slamming doors. They need love and loving discipline from you. Do they go to the counselor willingly?

Sharon: Yes, thankfully. Johnny tells me he likes Mike, his counselor.

Stephanie: You're lucky. My boys won't go to a counselor at all, even the school counselor. And I'm having a lot of problems with them swearing, back talking, staying out late, and refusing to do chores.

Renee: My children are adults, but they've suffered, too. The father they thought was a good man turned out to be evil. He is not a role model and he lied to them every day. They were shattered too. Sometimes, I guess you have to realize your father isn't always a role model.

Debbie: My kids are a bit older too, but their father turned out to be an alcoholic who cares little about our family. I feel awful about that.

Renee: I feel terrible also. All I wanted was to have a great family, yet the man I married and chose to be my kids' father turned out to be a cheating, lying, exploiter of women.

Stephanie: And I married an alcoholic. Now my sons treat me like their father treated me. I feel like I chose a bad father, and now my kids have learned how to be jerks too. And it's my fault.

Debbie: I've had back talk too, especially from my younger daughter, and it stems from the crappy father she has. I've told her many times I'm so sorry I picked the wrong man to marry.

Pat: I know it's hard to hear this, but I don't recommend you badmouth the children's father. They will become more confused by this, and often turn on you to defend their father. It's best to stay as neutral as possible in your comments. A child or adolescent doesn't benefit from hearing you married the wrong man. Again, keep your children in therapy with a skilled counselor so they can talk about issues and concerns they have with the divorce or with their father's treatment of them. Things work out much better in the long run if they come to terms with their father based on their own experiences with him rather than your comments.

Renee: I've also apologized that I married the man who became their rotten father. They deserved a good man as a father. That's on me. I chose him and then I enabled him because I thought I should keep trying and hoping. I didn't cause his disgusting behavior, but I also didn't demand he spend more time at home or hire a private investigator and get a divorce twenty years ago.

Debbie: But we didn't even know what enabling was.

Renee: Right. But now I know, and I feel crappy about it. I find it hard to acknowledge that my kids have a horrible father, and even harder to acknowledge that I, their mother, didn't stand up to him. The virtues I thought I had—patience, hope, and flexibility—I now see as weaknesses.

Pat: All of your children have been exposed to models of bad behavior from their fathers. Do not allow your kids to disrespect you, but don't get into shouting matches either. I know it's hard, Stephanie, but walk away. Say in a regular tone of voice, "Don't talk to me that way," and then leave the room. You can go to your room and softly close the door. Your sons, Stephanie, must learn how to speak to you in respectful ways. You will have to be firm and know this may take a while. They saw such disrespect from your ex and now they have to unlearn that behavior. You have to set boundaries for the behavior you will not tolerate.

Stephanie: I'm worried they'll treat their girlfriends badly too.

Pat: They might. But at least you divorced their father and they won't be hearing him call you names and seeing him mistreat and abuse you anymore, at least not to your face. Keep telling them at calm opportunities that you will not be disrespected; that you want them to be good men and treat all women with respect.

Stephanie: They witnessed bad behavior for years, and I let it go on far too long.

Pat: But you stopped it. That part of your life is over and you got a divorce. You have stopped the abuse. They have seen that too. They saw you becoming a strong woman, and you're not going to be disrespected any more. I can't recommend enough that you go to Al Anon and your sons attend Al A Teen. Their meetings will help all of you detach from the past and focus on things that are in your power now and in the future.

Renee: Al Anon helped me in many ways, but I still can't get over feeling guilty for the pain my kids endured.

Pat: But you didn't prostitute women. You didn't cheat on your husband.

Renee: No, but I enabled him by making accommodations that allowed him to get away with it. I feel almost like an accomplice to his behavior, and that is why I'm making amends now.

Stephanie: How?

Renee: I tell my kids I love them all the time. I try to be a great mother now. And for the women my husband degraded with my enabling, I'm doing work with my church to bring awareness to the problem of human trafficking.

Debbie: That's good. I tell my kids I love them all the time too, and I keep busy with volunteer work.

Pat: Yes, shower your kids with love, but set boundaries and continue to discipline with love. Renee, enabling does not mean you were an accomplice. So please don't take on that guilt.

Sharon, make sure your kids see their counselor after every visit with your ex so they can report anything bad that might happen. The counselor will file another 51A and call the police if necessary.

To all of you: your narcissistic and sociopathic husbands do not feel guilt for all the damage and pain they caused. Yet, all of you feel guilt—which is why they married you. They knew you were people they could take advantage of and manipulate. You feel guilty for their behavior, even for enabling their behavior, but that guilt is misplaced. You can regret you married them. With that regret, learn the warning signs so you don't get involved with a narcissistic abuser again. That is in your control.

Reader: Yikes. The divorces are done, but the emotions are still boiling over.

Session Forty-One

Regret: Why Did I Wait So Long?

Pat: During the last session, you all shared that you feel awful about your marriages and blame yourselves for the pain your kids feel. Sharon, you also feel bad about how much your mother has been involved. Stephanie, you're having a hard time with your sons. Tonight I want to talk about the difference between guilt and regret.

Stephanie: I guess I don't understand how guilt and regret are different.

Pat: The difference does exist, and it's important for you to understand. Feeling guilty comes from doing something you knew was wrong. Regret is the feeling that comes from later learning you could possibly have done something better. Regret appears when you have more information later to assess your situation.

Renee: Why is it so important that we know the difference?

Pat: Because you describe yourselves as feeling guilty about choosing these men as your husbands and having a part in enabling their behavior.

193

Renee: Well, we did.

Pat: But you did not knowingly decide to marry alcoholics, narcissists, sociopaths, abusers, cheaters, or liars, right?

Sharon: Of course not. But why is that important?

Pat: When you married these men, you didn't know the things you know now. That means you can regret not knowing these things before you married, but you've all taken the bold step of divorce and the hard work of healing. Guilt causes self-blame and can paralyze you and lead to depression. Please don't own, or take responsibility for, things you couldn't do anything about.

You have enough on your plates. This is your time to blossom, not fold into depression. So please keep reminding yourselves that you regret marrying these men, but don't feel guilty about it.

Stephanie: My husband says he regrets marrying me.

Pat: Don't pay any attention to what he says about you. He no longer matters to you, and he's just saying that to hurt you.

Sharon: I'm confused about how regret or guilt about our husbands carries over onto my children.

Pat: What do you mean?

Sharon: I mean, I'm so happy I have my children. I love them so much, and I wouldn't have them if I hadn't married the creep who is their father.

Pat: This is important, and it's another reason you must separate guilt from regret. You are all devoted mothers. When you married and had children, you had no idea your husbands would turn out the way they did. When you found out, you tried different things, but finally realized divorce was the only solution. Does it make sense to regret your marriages, but not regret your children? Yes it does. I hear many women say their children are the only good that came out of their marriages. So, lavish your children with love and let them know how happy you are that they are your children. No regrets there, and certainly no guilt that they were born. Is this getting any clearer?

Debbie: What about the person who says he has no regrets? I heard an actor say that on TV.

Pat: It's a pithy phrase, but not realistic. If a person lives with no regrets, you should wonder how many of life's lessons that person learned, or how honestly he or she is able to look at themselves.

Stephanie: What about shame? I think my sons feel ashamed, because their parents are divorced and their father is an alcoholic.

Pat: I'm glad you brought that up. It's important for you and your kids not to feel shame for what your husbands did. Shame results when you think you deserved to be treated badly. This can happen after long periods of physical, verbal, or sexual abuse. None of you deserved to be yelled at, called names, lied to, hit, choked, ridiculed, thrown out of cars, and cheated on. Your children did not deserve to be yelled at, neglected, hit, or sexually molested. They did not deserve having an alcoholic or sex addicted father. They did not deserve fathers who treated their mothers so badly that their moms worked on coping instead of thriving.

Stephanie: My kids are not doing well at all.

Debbie: My kids have a lot of issues too.

Renee: My children are hurting, each one dealing with it in a different way. I'm certainly not the mother I want to be—a strong, wise rock.

Pat: Yes, you are. Listen, all your children need to have counselors who can assure them that, while life has dealt them a bad card hand, they have nothing to be ashamed about, and they have the rest of their life to chart their own paths.

Renee: Will there be a quiz on all this? My head hurts.

Pat: Very funny. I want you to think about the distinctions among guilt, regret, and shame. The people who should feel guilt and shame— your husbands—probably don't. Don't expect them to, either. You can regret your past actions, but now love your kids and yourselves and work on making the future better for all of you. You and your children have nothing to be ashamed about!

Reader: I'm sure it's hard to not feel some guilt or shame, but I hope these wonderful women will learn to stop blaming themselves and feel more regret than guilt.

Session Forty-Two

Raising Children as a Single Mom

Setting Boundaries and Rules

Pat: Stephanie and Sharon are having challenges with their kids, so let's talk about raising kids as a single mom.

Sharon: I always wanted children, but I wanted them to have a father and a mother.

Debbie: Yeah, me too.

Pat: You'll find millions of single parent families in this country, and they can be happy. Let's focus on what works best in these situations. You probably received tips in the parenting classes ordered by your judges, but those teachers seldom discuss how to parent with an unreliable and manipulative alcoholic, a violent abuser, or someone suspected of molesting the children.

Stephanie: I feel like my precious children have grown up to be selfish, disrespectful teenagers.

Renee: How do you tell the difference between normal, obnoxious teen behavior, versus behavior that comes from living in a dysfunctional home?

Pat: Good question. Preteens and teens always test the limits with their parents. You should be worried if your child, especially a teenager, is completely obedient all the time. That said, parents should have several tools in their toolbox. Sharon will have different rules and expectations for her young children when they're with her than her ex will have at his home. Sharon will need to let her children decompress when they return from visits with their father. Most children need a re-entry time period when they return back from visitation.

Stephanie, you need to tell your teenage sons you have new ground rules since they're older and the divorce is done. They need to know you will not tolerate verbal abuse. Those days are gone. Try and be consistent and stand by what you say you'll do if they violate your rules. I know this can be a tough, bumpy road to travel, but you can do it!

Stephanie: They don't listen.

Pat: Tell them again and again that you love them, but they may not yell at you, swear in the house, slam doors, hurt other people, or wreck anything. Tell them what you expect for chores, because you're still a family and need to work together. Be clear about your expectation. If they neglect their assigned chores, don't shout at them, but don't do the chores yourself.

Stephanie: My sons won't do any chores, or at least not well and not without a lot of griping.

Pat: If the chore isn't done, then you can't drive them to the mall or a friend's house. Tell them why and walk away. Do not negotiate. Do not engage with an irrational teenager who will be whining, yelling, or stomping around. Leave the room. It may take several of these temper outbursts, but they will get the message. And resist the need to say something like, "Now that wasn't so bad," or anything like that. Just tell them, "Thank you," when the work is done. The less talk the better.

Stephanie: What do I do with all the poison my ex tells the boys about me?

Pat: Give me an example.

Stephanie: He tells them he has no money because I have it all, that I wrecked the family, and we're all poor because of me.

Pat: Obviously your ex tuned out the part of parenting classes where they said not to put the kids in the middle.

Stephanie: Exactly.

Pat: Your sons are old enough for you to be straight with them. They're old enough to know there is less money and you all need to pull together. They may howl about movie night at home, but do it anyway and keep inviting them. At some point, one of your sons will plop down on the couch with you, maybe even with a friend. Make popcorn. Watch the movie and be goofy. Teenagers hate silly parents, and you can tell them you know that. That's why you're doing it. They need to see you smile, and that being with them makes you smile.

Stephanie: I can almost hear the ridicule coming out of their mouths.

Pat: Maybe so, and if it's verbal abuse, say so and leave the room. If it's an attempt for them to be silly too, go with the flow. But if you are called stupid, or b----, or any name like that, then immediately leave the room.

Stephanie: See what you can look forward to, Sharon?

Sharon: I have my hands full already, and I'm still taller than my children!

Pat: Sharon, it's important for you to be clear about the rules when they're home with you, especially when they are wild at their father's home. Some of the rules are the same as before—like no backtalk, no hitting or shoving—all that sort of stuff. Keep them doing chores and give lots of praise and thanks when they do their part. That goes for all of you, even with young adult children. They will always be your children.

Renee: I call my 27 year old Sugey Boo, just to be silly and affectionate. One of his roommates read a card from me with Dear Sugey Boo written on it. The roommate now calls my son Sugey Boo. When my son told me about it, he was smiling.

Debbie: That's sweet. But I've had to be very tough with my younger eighteen year old daughter. She was talking back to me a lot, and I told her that was unacceptable. Then she told me she couldn't stand being home anymore, so she packed a bag and went to a friend's house. She never called, but I guessed where she went and I called the mom over there. Her friend's mom said it was fine if she stayed there awhile. I got through it.

Stephanie: Oh, no. How long did she stay away?

Debbie: It was a long time—about five weeks.

Stephanie: I don't know if I could handle that.

Debbie: She's 18 now, and I kept checking that she was safe. She had a lot of things to think about, and her friend's parents had an extra room. Of course, my daughter behaved well over there, or she would have been told to leave. I think she just needed to be away for a little while.

Stephanie: What happened next?

Debbie: She came home one day—just opened the door and said, "I'm back." I told her "I'm glad you're back." I gave her a hug. She took her bag of clothes to her room. Later, I asked her if she wanted to go get groceries with me and she said yes. Life goes on. My older daughter isn't a problem like this at all. Is it more common for younger children to act out?

Pat: Age can make a difference, as well as the sex of the child. Maybe your younger daughter was more upset because she was younger when your husband left home. Sons and daughters each have their ways to act out when they're unhappy. Sometimes sons can miss a father figure and try to step in as the man of the house. They may try to assert that you don't have authority over them. But you are all strong women. Your kids need to see that you made it through the divorce, you're still their moms, and you can laugh and smile. Fake it till you make it! But never forget who is boss. They will complain, but they want discipline and they need it. And don't beat yourselves up when you forget and yell. Just do better next time.

Debbie: When my daughters try to pick a fight with me, I say, "I love you too much to fight with you." And then I walk away. Sometimes I look back and see them staring at me with their mouths open. It's actually funny at the time.

Stephanie: Pat, before we leave tonight, I want to get your input on how mad I am at my ex when he puts me down to my boys. Sometimes I lose it and tell the boys their dad is such a no good jerk. I feel bad, but I just need to vent and lash out.

Pat: I get how you feel and how you need to vent. But, I want to add that you should try very hard not to say bad things about your ex to your children.

Stephanie: Why not? Why shouldn't they know he's a drunken bastard who cares only about himself, and that he's the one who tore the family apart—not me?

Pat: Your kids do know this Stephanie. They lived it, and they don't need to be continually reminded of It.

Stephanie: So why can't I vent? It's my house.

Pat: This is important and difficult. We'll talk more about this in our individual sessions. But, for now, however justified and understandable your hurt and anger are toward your ex, when you bad mouth him to your kids, their natural reaction Is to defend him.

Stephanie: How can that be natural?

Pat: Because that drunken bastard, sociopathic liar, sex addict, or physical abuser is their father. They are half of him, and your attacks on him seem like attacks on them. What you hear back from them isn't a rational discussion about the faults and consequences of their fathers' action—it's a visceral, automatic reaction to defend their dads. You will set up the dynamics for more back talk and yelling at you. Most of your children have experienced some good times with their fathers and that's what they reflect on when you're berating and putting down their fathers. They say to themselves, "He's not that bad; what is her problem?"

You know the expression, "bite your tongue?"

Sharon: No.

Stephanie: Yes.

Pat: It means that no matter how hard it is, don't say anything. Don't complain or even mumble about what a good for nothing your ex is. Your sons know about the times he didn't show up, the fact that he acted like a drunken loud mouth jerk, and the fact that he still bad mouths you. They know and they are hurting.

Stephanie: Can I say anything?

Pat: Yes, you can say things like, "I decided to leave your father because I didn't want to be verbally insulted and put down by him." That is a statement of fact, not an insult or berating of their father. If your son is upset about something his father has said or done to him, like not showing up for a visitation or only talking about himself and his new girlfriend rather than asking about your son's wellbeing—in those cases when your son is complaining about his dad, you can say, "I know it's hard when he disappoints you that way." Or, "I understand how that would make you angry or upset." You can even go so far as to say, "You deserve for someone to treat you well and follow through on their promises to you. You're a wonderful young man and you deserve to be treated with kindness and respect."

Stephanie: What do I say when the boys complain that our lack of money is all my fault?

Pat: Say, "I'm sorry we don't have much money for now. I hope things will get better." Say nothing at all about their father. Practice, rehearse, and practice again. This won't be easy, but in the long run, the less you insult and berate their father, the more likely all your children will judge their fathers on their own experiences. They will judge these men on their merits and demerits, not on your verbal insults. You will need to bite your tongue often. But, I'm sure it will get easier, especially after you begin to see your children being objective and recognizing when their father is disrespectful to you or them.

Also, you're showing your children how reasonable adults should behave. If you lower yourself to your ex-husband's level, then your kids are dealing with two difficult, angry parents.

Stephanie: I may actually have to bite my tongue off.

Pat: Practice the phrase, "Bite my tongue," or, "I will not speak evil about their father," and when you find you have to say it, walk out of the room so you aren't tempted to say more. I assure you, the dynamic will eventually change with your sons, but it will take time. You can do this.

Stephanie: This isn't fair!

Pat: You're right, but it's the reality you're living with. I promise things will get better, especially when you learn not to emotionally respond with anger and hatred towards your ex in front of your children. You can always bring your anger here, into this room, with all of us.

Reader: Biting your tongue over insults would be so hard. I'm glad these women have a place to vent with each other. Being a mother after a divorce is difficult. What about the fathers?

Session Forty-Three

The Disney Dad Syndrome

Pat: How is everyone tonight?

Sharon: I'm still having problems with my kids and their father.

Pat: Does he still want joint legal custody and regular visitation?

Sharon: Yes, that's the biggest issue. But I also have a question that's really bugging me.

Pat: What?

Sharon: He no longer has any rules at his house as long as they don't bother him. He lets them do whatever they want while he's in the next room watching golf or some other sports event. The kids come home wild and spoiled. I never thought this would be a problem, because he was like a prison guard before the divorce.

Pat: Do you think this is a tactic?

Sharon: Yes. He knows if the kids tell their counselor he touches them, he'll have to deal with another investigation. So he stopped touching

205

them, which is good, of course, but from the time my mom drops the kids off at his house, they run around, snack when they want to, and stay in the Kids Room he set up with a couch, a TV, and a game console. He doesn't monitor anything. According to my son Johnny, their father mostly stays in his bedroom watching TV or working at his computer. The next day, they return home hyper and cranky. They haven't brushed their teeth or combed their hair. They go to bed whenever they want to. And he just announced he's taking them to Disney World for their next school vacation.

Debbie: Do your children still resist going to his house?

Sharon: No, they seem to be resigned to it and they enjoy being wild. It reminds me of Lord of the Flies.

Pat: I don't know about that, but I agree with you that this is a tactic. Since the investigation by DCF, he's smart enough not to inappropriately touch your children. Instead, he does the bare minimum of parenting.

Sharon: Is this problem unique to me?

Pat: Not at all. In fact it has a name: the Disney Dad Syndrome. In your case, it's aptly named since he can actually afford a Disney trip.

Sharon: Why is this a syndrome?

Pat: Many divorced fathers have their kids for a short period of time. Some dads feel guilty about the divorce and try to compensate by lavishing the kids with gifts and vacations. Many of these men never really parented their children before the divorce, so they plan big activities to keep the kids busy because they don't know how to have quiet time or play time with the children.

Your husbands also may have no clue about placing limits on behavior. Spoiling the kids is often their substitute for love, or actually spending time with the kids on other projects or school activities. A Disney dad rarely helps with homework assignments or drives his children to and from events. The kids get spoiled by the gift giving and lack of rules, rather than authentic one-on-one time with a parent.

Sharon: Anything else I should know?

Pat: Yes, and I think this is happening in your case. Your ex-husband is competitive. He wants to be the fun parent and saddle you with the disciplinary role. He may also be buying the kids' affection with gifts and fun trips, because he may be planning to ask for more time with them. At a future hearing for full co-parenting, the kids will be receptive to it. He's manipulating the kids to get to you.

Sharon: Oh, no! He is not a good parent. He neglects the kids.

Pat: I agree. What you've described verges on neglect. I'm sure he feeds them, but otherwise he leaves them to their own devices rather than spending quality time with them. Are they still seeing the counselor?

Sharon: Yes, and they're now dealing with school issues. They don't do their homework at their father's house and they think they can do whatever they want.

Pat: Make sure the counselor knows how unstructured and unsupervised the time with their father is. You're lucky to have such a good psychologist for them.

Stephanie: I believe a similar thing is going on with my teenage sons at their father's apartment. There are no rules and he lets them drink and smoke pot.

Reader: Boy, this Disney Dad Syndrome makes these guys sound like real Goofy type jerks. I think a better name for them is Dismal Dads!

Session Forty-Four

The Other Mother

Pat: Shall we continue our discussion from last time about how hard it is to parent your children?

Stephanie: Oh, yeah. After all our talk last week about how disrespectful my son is to me, he tells me he's decided to enlist in the Army. I can't believe it.

Debbie: What's wrong with that?

Stephanie: I think he's running away from home. From me! It is breaking my heart. And I'm afraid he'll get hurt or killed.

Pat: I agree with you that he may want to get away, but maybe you can tell us more about why your son has decided to enlist in the Army rather than continue with school.

Stephanie: Sure. Brian was flunking out of his classes at community college and they put him on academic probation. He never told me. Anyway, he dealt with failing grades by partying more. Then he got pulled over by a cop for speeding, so he has to pay for the ticket and his insurance will increase. His part time job at the store won't be enough and he asked me for money. When I told him I didn't have money for this, he called me a crazy b— and stormed out of the house. He's with his father now.

Pat: I am sorry, Stephanie. This all must be difficult for you. It's not acceptable for him to expect you to be his bank when he gets in trouble. Being with his father may be for the best at the moment. He'll have time to cool off and it gives you a respite from his badgering. You'll have space for a moment, but I don't think it will last long. When he asks to come back, let him know you'd love for him to come back and live with you again—if he's willing to follow your rules.

Stephanie: But what about the Army? He told me he enlisted and he'll be leaving in September. Is he trying to punish me?

Pat: Not necessarily. He may be looking to get away, but he also may realize he's getting nowhere hanging out with his friends and partying. Maybe he knows he needs discipline from outside to get his life back on track. And who knows, he may really be patriotic and want to serve his country. You can tell him you're worried for his safety and don't want him to leave because you're his mom, but you support his decision and you'll help him get ready as much as you can. This may turn out to be a good thing for him. In the end, he's old enough to enlist and he did. College isn't his path, at least for now.

Stephanie: I have to think this through. He did tell me something about needing to get out of here because he thinks he's going nowhere fast, and the Army might help.

Pat: Maybe it will help if you call the recruitment office for general information about what's involved in joining the Army.

Sharon, what about your kids?

Sharon: My kids told me last weekend their dad had a lady there. I couldn't believe it.

Debbie: Boy, he sure moves fast. Reminds me of my ex.

Renee: Yeah, like my ex. He was dating right away and is now remarried. I don't care; let her have him and his craziness.

Pat: Sharon, did the children give you any details?

Sharon: Yes, Johnny gave me all the details. The lady was pretty, she read them stories, and she made ravioli for dinner. That's one of their favorites. He even said she smelled good.

Pat: Are you upset that your ex is dating?

Sharon: I don't feel one bit of jealousy about him dating. I don't love him at all, and I don't care if he dates and even remarries. You told us narcissists usually date again quickly, because they need someone to adore them, give them power, and let them be in control. I think he's also trying to say, "Look at me, I'm dating. See, you're the loser. Other women love me." But, I am actually happy because she's distracting him from tormenting me.

Pat: Right, and statistics show that men usually start dating and remarry sooner than women after a divorce or death of a spouse. This is probably because men are needier in terms of caretaking, as well as needing a sexual partner.

Sharon, why are you crying?

Sharon: I can't stand to think about that woman making my children their favorite dinner, reading stories to them, and that they liked her. I want them to hate her!

Debbie: Oh, no, Sharon. Here's some Kleenex. I feel for you. Does it help if I hate her? This must be hard.

Sharon: I can't handle another thing. He's doing this just to torture me. If they call her mom, I will just die.

Pat: Wait a minute, Sharon. You're jumping the gun. They just started dating. Having your ex dating someone who is now being a mommy figure to your children is hard to deal with. But, this is early in the relationship and it may not develop into anything. If it does continue, please realize you can get through it.

Sharon: I don't want another woman there when my children are visiting.

Pat: You can't control his dating unless it hurts your children in some way. I don't recommend introducing your children to new people you're dating unless you're been seeing each other awhile, like six months, and believe this person is a partner to whom you're committed. Unfortunately, many people introduce their children too soon, only to have the children experience another loss when the parent breaks up with the new partner. If you ex is dating someone nice, you can hope she will be kind to your children and be a good buffer with your ex.

Sharon: Okay, but that's all. She can be nice to my children, but I don't want them to love her. I'll go crazy if she tries to be their mother!

Pat: We'll talk more about this at our individual session on Thursday, but for now, please listen.

Your children will never replace you with their father's girlfriend or even a new wife—no matter how nice she is. You are their mom and they love you and you love them. They will not replace you. In all my years of practice, I've never seen children reject a loving mother for a step mother. If you continue to be the loving, supportive mom they've always known, you will always be their mother. You will not be replaced by a step-mother or girlfriend. In fact, if she's a nice woman, she may actually benefit you as a go-between for you and your ex. So the best thing you can do right now is to stay calm and continue being a loving, nurturing mom to your children.

Sharon: Thanks, Pat. I needed to hear I won't be replaced. I'm still afraid, but I'll just keep being the best mom I can be.

Reader: I can see why Sharon is scared about losing her young children to another mother. All these women try so hard to be good moms, but they keep getting dumped on.

Session Forty-Five

It's Your Fault, Mom!

Pat: Hi everyone. What would you like to talk about today?

Stephanie: Right now, my biggest problem is having my youngest son blaming me for everything.

Debbie: What does he say?

Stephanie: Jay says "We can't do anything anymore." "I'm the only kid at school who doesn't have his own car... or new sneakers... or a class ring." Or whatever.

Debbie: You know that's not true—right?

Stephanie: I know plenty of kids at the high school don't have their own cars and the latest sneakers, but a lot of my children's friends have these things, so I feel guilty.

Renee: Remember, you are not the abuser and the alcoholic.

Stephanie: I know, I know. I think my ex convinced them that getting a divorce was selfish on my part—that if we stayed married the

213

family wouldn't be poor. So they think it's all about me. I am miserable. And now I'm sure I'll be hearing that my older son is joining the Army because I'm such a bad mother.

Pat: Stephanie, you are a good mother, and joining the Army may be the best thing for your older son. Keep repeating to yourself and your sons that the divorce was necessary to stop the abuse. Period. No discussion. No guilt on your part, please. Do not accept their attempts to blame you for their father being an alcoholic and abusing you. Tell them you love them and all you can do is to be the best you can be now, and together you and your sons will make things better for the future. Leave the room and go for a walk. They may not understand this now, or maybe they refuse to remember how things were with the shouting and insults and meanness in your house. Most teenagers see themselves as the center of the universe. They will mature, but along the way, they may yell and say awful things. Keep repeating to yourself, "It not my fault, it is not my fault,"–and go to Al Anon. You will learn how blame and guilt sucks the oxygen from a home with an alcoholic in it. You stopped that by getting the divorce. Go, Stephanie!

Reader: I feel so frustrated! These women, who do 90% or more of the work raising their children, end up being blamed by their kids for the divorce.

Session Forty-Six

Financial Survival

Pat: Tonight, let's talk about money, or the lack thereof.

Stephanie: You've got that right.

Pat: I want to address this, because each one of you faced a different financial situation before and after divorce, and I think we can share tips with each other. From individual therapy with many women, I realize money is a huge problem in divorces. In fact, money keeps thousands of women in terrible marriages because they don't want to face the stress of a financial crisis brought on by divorce. You all took the strong, brave step toward a healthier life, but maybe temporarily a poorer one. So, would you like to spend some time on this topic tonight?

Stephanie: Yes. Every day I worry about money. It drains my energy, but unless someone gives me a winning lottery ticket, I don't think there's much to talk about.

Debbie: Divorce leaves both sides poorer, right?

Sharon: I'm not poor. I have alimony, unless I remarry. I haven't worked outside the home since my kids were born. My biggest asset out

215

of the divorce is the house. I'd like to sell it and move far away, but I can't move far away with shared legal custody. My ex won't let me. My kids' counselor also said to not sell the house right away anyway, because my kids need the stability of being in the same house for a while. The alimony should cover my expenses, as long as he pays it.

Debbie: Does he?

Sharon: So far, yes. The check comes from his company; so he doesn't personally write a check every month.

Debbie: Cheater has not paid me what he owes, and I have to go to court to threaten him with contempt and force him to pay. So not only is money tight, but it costs hundreds of dollars in lawyer fees each time.

Pat: Is he able to pay you?

Debbie: Yes.

Pat: Then it's another way of trying to hurt or punish you. Your former husbands are angry and they use your children, alimony, or both, to get back at you.

Stephanie: Well, it's working in my case. I got our house in the settlement too, but I don't make enough money to pay all the bills. I'm completely dependent on him, even after the divorce. I need to make arrangements to get his check from the Department of Revenue, so I can get it in time to pay the mortgage.

Renee: Can you increase your hours at the store?

Stephanie: I've asked, but they won't make me full time. In fact, the store cut my hours from 30 to 20 hours a week, and I've had to miss work a few times because of court dates and other crises.

Renee: That's not good. Can you get a second job or a new job?

Stephanie: That's what I'll have to do, but working full time will mean less time at home with my sons. And I'm so tired.

Debbie: Stephanie, do your sons have jobs? I've told my kids they have to get jobs.

Stephanie: Both my sons are on sports teams and they need time for their school work. School isn't easy for either of them. My older son Brian basically flunked out of his first year at college and now has a small part time job. He needs to work more hours. I mentioned getting a job to Jay, the one still in high school, but he says: "If Dad was still here, I wouldn't need to work." So they both throw it back at me.

Pat: Again, your husband is telling them to blame you and he's avoiding responsibility for his own actions. Is he abusive toward them or drunk when they visit him?

Stephanie: No, I don't think he's abusive to them. But he does let them stay over on weekends with their buddies, and I know they're drinking. I think their Dad is either in his own room passed out or out at a bar with his secretary. Brian, my oldest, wants to live with his father until he reports to the Army.

Pat: So maybe he can't take them to Disney World like Sharon's ex-husband, but he lets them get away with things to "befriend" them. And he acts better around them now than he did before the divorce. Naturally, sons want to believe in their fathers. Brian is 18 now—right? If he wants to live with his father, let him. I predict it won't last long. And since he's been awful to you, getting him out of your house may be a good thing. If and when he wants to come back, welcome him but be clear about the rules.

Stephanie: My ex's family is helping him out, just like my parents and sister helped me. But my family isn't wealthy. His parents are taking the boys and my ex on a cruise after school ends in June.

Pat: Do not compare your life with their lives. You love your sons. Tell them that and try to smile and let them know you're glad they have these opportunities with their grandparents.

Stephanie: I'm not glad, but I'll pretend. What am I going to do about money?

Renee: Can you sell the house or refinance?

Stephanie: I can do that in about three months, but I'll need somewhere to live.

Debbie: Maybe you can scope out the real estate market now so you know what's available. Maybe even get a condo. In the meantime, can you have a tag sale? I'll come and help you.

Stephanie: Maybe the tag sale will be for my sons' spending money. That could make them part with some stuff.

Pat: I know it's difficult for you, but speak to each of your sons again to explain that the divorce was necessary for your safety, and you need their help if they want spending money. I think they'll eventually step up to the plate and get jobs. If they don't, they don't. You took the steps you needed. It sounds like selling the house is a good option. Many women don't want to move, while others can't wait to move.

Stephanie: I'm in the middle. I know I can't keep up the house by myself. Plus, it's filled with bad memories. I'm just exhausted, and I know getting the house ready to sell will be a lot of work. I also don't have any money to make any repairs or spruce things up. If I ask the boys to help, I just get dumped on more.

Pat: When you decide to sell your house, make sure you get a good broker. Ask around, just like when you hired a lawyer. You need someone who understands your situation and won't strap you in a new home you cannot afford.

Before you decide to sell, make sure you can find another place that will cost less. Sometimes your mortgage may be low enough that it's better to stay put. I know some single women who take in boarders from the local colleges. They have female grad students who are in the occupational therapy program or physician's assistant program—students who need to study a lot. Renting a room helps the women pay their mortgages, so you might check into that before giving up your house that has a low mortgage. And meanwhile, keep your eyes open for job opportunities. You have a degree with job skills, and you've had steady employment in the past.

Reader: I see that divorce has a huge ripple effect. When do these ladies get to move on?

MOVING ON

Session Forty-Seven

Taking Care of Yourself

Lifelines and Survival Tips

Pat: We've been meeting for almost a year, and you've all provided great support for each other through these tough weeks and months. I've often reminded you about staying healthy by caring for yourselves, mind, body, and spirit. In the book, *The Body Keeps Score*, Bessel Van Der Kolk says that in order to heal from trauma, we must bring mindfulness to our bodies, thoughts, and emotions by using therapy, relaxation strategies like yoga, and learning to take control of our lives. I thought today we might put together a list of divorce survival tips—lifelines for other women who are going through what you survived so they can gain some control of their lives . Let's collectively list your strategies:

* Have a safe house or houses and people you can call if you need to flee quickly at any time, day or night.

* Change the locks on your house as soon as your lawyer says it's okay.

* Make a copy of your house key for a nearby trusted friend or neighbor.

* If you get a restraining order against your husband, tell the police so they know in case he shows up. The police may also be able to give you a Do Not Trespass order.

* Have a readily available copy of the separation or divorce decree related to custody and visitation, in case you need to call the police about a violation. Police officers may ask to see your legal papers.

* Break off direct contact with your ex if he's a narcissistic sociopathic liar, a cheater, and a creep. Questions should go through your lawyers, even after the divorce is final. Use parenting apps for coordinating kids' activities.

* Jot down your thoughts, feelings, questions and to-do lists. Your short term memory may be weak while you're under stress. Carry a notebook in your purse and car.

* Listen to your attorney and don't hesitate to ask questions so you understand what's happening.

* Don't expect your attorney to be a magician who can turn your soon to be ex-husband into a rational being.

* Write about your thoughts and feelings in a notebook or journal. This can be cathartic.

* If you're experiencing anxiety or depression, call your doctor. These may be serious symptoms.

* If your doctor or therapist thinks you may be experiencing post-traumatic stress, you may need to seek a specialist in PTSD treatment. Don't try to tough it out or go through this alone.

* Keep family traditions for yourself and your kids. You may have to downsize and make adjustments, but your family

needs some traditions to stay the same. You'll be tempted to just skip Christmas fuss, or Passover, but the effort is worth it when the rest of your family's world feels like it's in freefall.

*   Create new family traditions. Fresh starts are always good after you divorce.

*   Don't hesitate to say NO to requests to bake, chaperone, and volunteer. Say. "My plate is full right now," and don't feel guilty.

*   Or, say YES to some volunteer work if you can handle it. Helping others can be a break from your problems and make you feel good.

*   If the ex will be at events you want to attend, either go with someone else or sit with trusted friends. Ask a friend to walk with you to the car.

*   You need your sleep. Don't use electronic devices before bed, because their light stimulates wakefulness. If you're having sleep issues (and who wouldn't during a divorce?) try herbal tea and a hot bath or shower before bed. Also try to keep a consistent bedtime and wake up time; this will help get your body into a good sleep/wake cycle. If you still have trouble sleeping, contact your doctor to see if prescription medication would be helpful.

*   Take walks to think, blow off steam, and get exercise, all at the same time.

*   Go to a gym. Sign up for an exercise or yoga class or follow a fitness class on TV. Exercise and stretching help the body and mind.

*   Grow something. Raise flowers and other plants in your yard or in containers. Nurturing growing things helps soothe the soul.

*   Be careful! Literally watch your step. Stress can make you clumsy.

*   Simplify wherever you can. Misplacing and losing things is common. Place your keys in the same place every day.You are not losing your mind; you are under stress.

* Wear sunglasses and a hat or scarf to give yourself slack on your appearance.

* Ask for help from family, friends, and neighbors. You would help them if they were in need.

* Discard his pillow, bed sheets, even the whole marital bed if you can. Sleeping on a cheap mattress on the floor can be wonderful compared to trying to sleep on a bed of pain. Donate, throw out, or sell everything that reminds you of him. Declutter and simplify the home so it becomes *your* home.

* Rearrange the furniture to change your home as your life is changing. A can of paint works wonders.

* If your kids need sports equipment you can't afford, ask family and friends. You'll be surprised how much left over and out grown equipment is lying around other peoples' houses. Tag sales are important too. You won't be in this position forever.

* If you can't afford to pay for school activities, events, and bus transportation, call your school counselor or principal to waive the fees. They do this all the time.

* Make sure your kids' schools know about the divorce and the custody issues. They should know who's permitted to pick up your kids at school. You are not responsible for keeping your ex informed of school events; he is. The parenting apps are helpful.

* When your children complain about life after divorce, tell them you love them and things will get better as you work through this adjustment time.

* Seek out Al Anon or another support group if your divorce involves an addiction.

* Talk about topics other than your divorce with your friends. The divorce shouldn't monopolize every conversation.

* If someone wants to tell you about seeing your ex somewhere, say, "I quit that job, so let's talk about __ (anything) instead."

* Escape with good books and movies on TV. Avoid sad media or anything that reminds you of him. For now, seek entertainment that uplifts you and makes you laugh. Go to the library to borrow books, movies, and music for free, or ask to borrow from friends and family.

* Keep detailed records of visitation time drop offs and pick-ups and missed times. Also keep a record of emails and phone calls.

* Call the police if you feel threatened in any way. Getting offenses on record with the police will help you in court, so it isn't just hearsay.

* Once you file for divorce anything financial freezes, and you can't do anything except routine expenses. Think about that before you file for the divorce. Assume he is hiding money, receipts, and other items he wants private. Your lawyer will request documents and information from him, and his lawyer will ask the same of you.

* Your name is your choice. Some women keep their married names so they share a last name with the children. Others go back to their maiden names, or add the maiden name to their married names. This is your choice, not his.

* If you know you're going to change to your maiden name after the divorce, start getting used to it early by using your maiden name as a middle name.

* Arrange to get support checks from the Department of Revenue or another source, not directly from him. Be sure you make this clear with your lawyer.

* As soon as your attorney gives the nod, close any bank accounts he can access.

* You may need a private investigator or computer forensic tech to find the extent of his philandering and other bad behavior. It is best if these things are ordered by your lawyer.

* You need to change the beneficiaries of your will and insurance policies, if allowed in the divorce settlement. You should remove his name as your healthcare proxy, because you certainly don't want him making decisions for your end of life medical care should you become incompetent. If you don't have these documents, ask your divorce attorney or another attorney. This is part of your new life.

* Fake it 'til you make it! Wear clean clothes, wash and style your hair, wear a fragrance, and try to smile, at least around your kids. Your children really, really need to see you smile at them.

* Make a list on an index card of your blessings and carry it in your wallet or purse. This is good to have on hand when you're having a bad day.

* Also have an index card that lists why you divorced your husband. This will help you remember why you made the decision to divorce, if and when you have doubts during tough times.

* Healing takes time. Be patient with yourself as you move through the process.

Reader: These suggestions could be life savers!

Session Forty-Eight

Letting Go of Anger

Pat: How is everyone feeling tonight?

Stephanie: Depressed.

Pat: What's up?

Stephanie: I look in the mirror and see a frazzled exhausted woman with dark circles under my eyes and tons of worries. I am so angry that I'm 46 years old and I wasted my life on a no good man who's still tied to me because of alimony and support. I could scream.

Pat: How do the rest of you feel about this?

Sharon: I feel like screaming too.

Renee: Me, too.

Pat: Before you all start screaming and someone down the hall calls the police, please know that I don't do primal scream therapy. But seriously, ladies, you've been through a lot. You are physically and emotionally exhausted, so no wonder sometimes you want to have a good scream or a good cry. Let it out. You aren't crazy to do this. Sometimes instead of singing in the shower you can use this as an opportunity to scream or cry. But please make sure your kids are not around at the time. Let's talk tonight about still being angry.

Renee: Are we not supposed to be angry anymore?

Sharon: My blood boils every time I think about my ex. I try to do something quickly to occupy my mind.

Pat: That is actually a good technique. You have every right to be angry. I call this righteous anger, because you've been done wrong, as the Country Western songs say. But you shouldn't dwell too much on anger because dwelling with anger causes disease, or ill health.

Stephanie: How can we not be angry?

Pat: Your anger is acceptable and perfectly understandable. You've all been betrayed by your husbands.

Stephanie: Who also stole the best years of our lives, hurt our kids, and cost a ton of money in lawyer fees which my parents had to help me pay.

Renee: I agree. And gave me anxiety attacks, PTSD, asthma, insomnia, hair loss, fibromyalgia, and last but not least—gonorrhea. And now the anxiety is back again.

Pat: Why?

Renee: On Monday I got a letter from my ex, forwarded by my lawyer, to announce he was going to stop paying the college loans for the kids. I had to read his awful letter telling me the loans are no longer his responsibility and last month's payment is overdue.

Debbie: Can he do that?

Renee: Unfortunately, yes. He paid what he owes on the loans under the divorce settlement.

Pat: So, you agreed to take over the loans in your settlement. And you knew this was coming.

Renee: I miscomputed. I thought his portion would be paid up about four months ago, so when I didn't hear anything, I hoped he decided to do the right thing.

Debbie: Wait. Why would paying more be the right thing for him if you agreed to something else?

Renee: My ex made all the financial decisions about the college tuition. In fact he yelled at me one night to stay out of it, because it would be his salary paying for all the loans. I only worked part time. I was also suggesting the kids go to in-state public colleges. He said what I thought didn't matter. Anyway, I did stay out of it to keep the peace. I didn't sign any of the loan agreements, and there are a lot of loans. In order to get to a divorce settlement, I agreed to pay a third of the loans out of my inheritance from my deceased brother. Then ex would pay the next third. The last third would come back to me and the kids who finished college. He's working, and I just hoped he'd step up to the plate and continue paying monthly on the loans. How horribly lucky I was to have any money at all because of my brother's death. And now I'll be paying the last third. I was just hoping he'd do the right thing.

Pat: Okay, I think I understand. You need to listen, Renee, and everyone else too. Hope snared you into thinking your marriages would get better if you kept working at it. This futile hope enabled your husbands to get away with horrendous behavior during your marriages. Now you're divorced. Stop hoping that your narcissistic, lying, cheating sociopathic ex-husbands will ever do the right thing. They will never do anything that does not give them immediate gratification. They did not care for you during your marriages and they don't care about you now. Assess the facts facing you now about the loans, Renee. Call the banks, figure out a plan, and then focus on making a better life for yourself and your kids.

Renee: I know, I know. I thought I'd moved on. I can usually veer my thoughts away from the bad times and focus on the present and the future. Now these loans are dumped back on me. I'll be paying for what he promised our children he'd do long ago, and I have a tight budget already. It makes me angry all over again.

Pat: Anger was the fuel that got you all through difficult divorces.

Debbie: I was on jet fuel.

Renee: Nuclear reactor fuel.

Pat: That's right. You all needed high octane fuel to get you through such contentious divorces. Now don't relive the unfairness and pain of your marriages or the divorces. You should expect periodic encounters or situations to pop up and remind you of the bad times. That is reality. But don't let it rekindle the anger.

Sharon: Will I ever feel normal?

Pat: That's a great question. First, what is normal? We've talked about this before.

Sharon: Well, I used to smile and laugh and sleep at night. I used to listen to music and go out and have fun. Then I met Mark, and my life took a dive soon after the wedding.

Pat: Look back, all of you, at the time before you even met your ex-husbands. I want for you all to make him as emotionally irrelevant to you as before you met him. Let it go. Let him go.

Renee: Go where? It's in our past.

Debbie: Can I get a lobotomy?

Pat: What I mean is, the chunk of your life that revolved around your ex-husband, is OVER. You can't forget it, but you can keep it in your past. It's in your rear view mirror. The past is past. The past doesn't exist in your present anymore; it is NOT happening now.

Debbie: It's not in my rear view mirror because of my lawsuit.

Stephanie: And I still get alimony.

Sharon: Me too, and child support.

Pat: The part to let go of is when he was your betraying husband and you tried to make a sick marriage work with an abusive, narcissistic sociopath who's addicted to alcohol, pornography, or whatever. Is that part, his being your husband, done for you, Stephanie?

228

Stephanie: Yes.

Pat: So you no longer have to walk around on eggshells worrying about his voice and his shoves.

Stephanie: At least not in my home.

Pat: That's right, and it's important. Sharon, the part about hearing him tell you what a bad mother you are and getting thrown out of your house and a moving car—all that's done, right?

Sharon: Yes. But I still worry about his threats to me and his behavior toward my kids.

Pat: It's good to be vigilant, but you are not alone Sharon. You have your mom, friends, your lawyer, the police, and everyone in this room.

Renee and Debbie, you're a bit older and had longer marriages. You're angry that your ex-husbands took away so many years of your lives and caused pain for your children.

Renee: The word anger doesn't half describe it.

Pat: But it's over. You aren't twisting yourself like pretzels trying to fix things with your ex-husbands anymore, right?

Debbie: Correct.

Renee: Yes.

Pat: So I repeat: Work on not letting those bad past chapters of your lives generate new anger. Each of you must have some dealings with your exes, but the bad stuff you endured because you were married to these creeps is over. Say good bye and good riddance to the bad marriage.

Stephanie: What do I do when I think about him choking me or calling me names? I don't want to think about it, but sometimes I do.

Pat: When those thoughts pop up, tell yourself, "He can't do that to me anymore. It's over." And find something positive to occupy your mind. Read a book, watch TV, or listen to music. Meditate. Call a friend. Have you heard the expression, "Count your blessings?"

Stephanie: Yes.

Sharon: Yes

Pat: That may sound hokey, but it works. You heard Renee mention it when we listed the practical tips. List your blessings on a sheet of paper or an index card and keep it with you, tape a copy to your mirror, and keep another one at your bedside. When bad thoughts happen—and they will—take out your blessings and read them. Add to the list as often as you can. You will shrink the bad stuff, while the positive people and things you have in your life will become more prominent in your thoughts. You'll stop looking out the rear view mirror, and instead start focusing on the road ahead. Whatever technique you decide to use, the longer you're safely away from him, the better you will feel about yourself and your emerging life. Save your energy for the present and future. YOUR present and YOUR future.

Reader: I didn't realize it takes a lot more than divorce to get over a bad marriage. Recovery takes work, but at least these ladies are finally working on themselves.

Session Forty-Nine

Must I Forgive Him?

Pat: Renee asked if we could talk about forgiveness, which is closely related to letting go. How did this come up, Renee?

Renee: From a sermon at church. Actually, I hear about forgiveness a lot. It feels like I'm surrounded by forgiveness mongering.

Pat: That's a strong statement. Do you feel like you're supposed to forgive your ex-husband?

Renee: Yes. Books, magazine articles, TV talk shows, TED Talks, and sermons at church are all about forgive, forgive, forgive.

Pat: And why is this a problem? You and I talked about this before, but I want to bring the group into the discussion.

Renee: People preach to us that forgiveness is good and necessary if we want to move on. And if I don't forgive, then I'm a cold, hard person who's also hurting herself. I want to move on, and I have moved on a lot, but I certainly don't feel like I've forgiven my ex for being a fraud father and a terrible husband. He hurt my body and my mind. He exploded our

231

family—and he isn't even sorry. How I am supposed to say, "Oh, that's okay. Would you like a hug?"

Pat: You're mixing condoning with forgiving.

Stephanie: What do you mean?

Pat: As far as I can see, none of you should ever condone what your husbands did to you. Absolutely not. Forgiving is different. Forgiving is letting go, and it's your choice, not to be determined by anyone else.

Debbie: I can talk about forgiveness. A lot has happened to me this past week. Greg called me and we talked.

Stephanie: Who's Greg?

Debbie: My ex-husband.

Stephanie: You mean Cheater? I didn't know he had a name!

Debbie: I'm going to call him Greg again.

Stephanie: Who are you and what have you done with Debbie?

Debbie: Very funny. I know this is big. He called a few days ago, and he was crying. He said the bank served him with foreclosure papers and all his accounts that were collateral have been frozen. He closed the restaurant. He's bankrupt.

Renee: What about his new wife, the massage lady?

Debbie: She walked out on him.

Stephanie: Karma is a bitch goddess.

Renee: Did you hang up on him?

Debbie: No, I listened. I think he bottomed out and I feel for him.

Renee: Maybe he's just feeling sorry for himself and manipulating you. Remember how these men operate.

Debbie: I don't think so. I think he's being real.

Stephanie: Did he ask you for money?

Debbie: No, and I wouldn't give him any if he did ask. I just feel some compassion. He said he'd go to AA meetings. He apologized for all the terrible things he's done to me.

Pat: He may have hit bottom, and he will need the support of AA to turn his life around. Be careful though, Debbie. It takes about two years of good sobriety and hard work for an alcoholic like your husband to be on a steady path. And he will be an alcoholic forever.

Debbie: I know that now. But I think I can forgive him. I had actually been thinking a lot about forgiveness before he called. I want to move on. There is a quote from Eckhart Tolle I found that has helped me a lot: "Sometimes letting things go is an act of far greater power than defending or hanging on."

Forgiving him is a gift from me to myself and is supposed to carry away the toxins I had against him. I feel better already. I regret the hatred I've carried for all these years. I need to move on, for me. Renee, you should work on this too, so you can release the poisons of hatred and get on with your life. I have a book about it I can lend you if you want.

Renee: You told him you forgave him? You wouldn't even say his name a week ago.

Debbie: I know you're in shock, but yes I did. He was sobbing.

Renee: Well, you are a saint, and I mean that. You're a better person than me. I'm not a saint, but I don't feel full of toxins either. I hate my ex and I feel bewildered that I'm expected to forgive him. Forgive him for buying and degrading and exploiting 650 women? For being addicted to porn and sex and lying to me and our children every day of our marriage? For a million acts of meanness? For giving me a disease?

Pat, you said my anger gave me energy to get through the divorce. Now I feel like I'm being judged for not being a good person, because if I was a good person, I could forgive. Al Anon is big on forgiveness and my religion is all about forgiveness. So what the heck is wrong with me? I want to ditch him in the past, but the thought of me telling him I forgive him makes me want to gag. I still don't feel safe from him.

Stephanie: You sound really churned up about forgiving or not. I don't forgive my ex, and I don't give it any thought. I think he's an alcoholic jerk and an awful person. I just don't care about him any more as long as he pays me as ordered by the divorce settlement. He's been a terrible father and role model, and all he taught my boys was how to be wretched toward me. I want as little to do with him as possible. I guess I don't worry that I'm a bad person because of these feelings. However, I do feel strongly that the bad karma he piled on me and my sons will come back at him. I'm not into religion, but I do believe you reap what you sow. It's not revenge, but when karma delivers bad stuff to his life—and she will—I won't feel sorry for my ex in the least. I may even smile. I think karma has found your Cheater, or Greg, or whoever he is.

Sharon: I also can't see the sense of me forgiving a man who threw me out the back door like a piece of garbage. I think he's molesting my kids, and he still threatens me. Forgiveness is not on my radar screen.

Pat: Nothing is wrong with any of you. I agree you're feeling great pressure to forgive, coming from friends, family, religion, and popular culture. But everyone responds and reacts differently when it comes to forgiving. Some people need to hear the offender say, "I'm sorry, can you forgive me?" Other people don't want to forgive at all, or they think it sounds artificial.

Renee: What do you mean by feeling artificial?

Pat: It feels artificial to forgive when you don't believe the other person has true, authentic contrition; or his apology wasn't sincere; or the apology was so global and general that it was only expressed to ease the offender's guilty conscience. And when you refuse the apology, sometimes manipulative people like your ex-husbands can make you feel like the offender. They say things like, "What's your problem? I said I was sorry—what more do you want?"

That's when your good girl tendencies kick in and you think something is wrong with you because you don't forgive. Yes, forgiveness is possible, but only when certain qualities are expressed by the offender.

Renee: What are they?

234

Pat: They are:

1. He must listen to the pain he caused you with an open and caring heart.

2. He must apologize genuinely and responsibly, not defensively.

3. He seeks to understand his behavior and reveals his character deficits to you.

4. He works diligently to earn back your trust.

5. He is able to forgive himself and be renewed.

These components of forgiveness can be explored and understood in the book *How Can I Forgive You?* by Janis Spring and Michael Spring.

Sharon: I can't deal with this now.

Pat: Don't feel badly that you aren't ready, willing, or able to forgive if your partner has never acknowledged his hurtful behavior and empathized with the pain he caused. Blanket apologies like, "I'm sorry if I ever did anything to hurt you," are only offered to let the offending party say, "See, I apologized." Rather he must ask you how he hurt you and listen attentively and with an open heart to understand your pain. If people can't do this, their behavior cannot change in a positive direction, because they don't have the courage to face the truth of their hurtful actions. Also, I encourage you to be cautious and not accept words alone; how the person acts and behaves is the best judge of change. A positive and long term change in behavior is the true sign of contrition and repentance.

Renee: Unlike Debbie, I don't want to have a conversation with my ex. I don't want to tell him about my pain and to listen to hear if he apologizes and then try to figure out if he's sincere or fake. I don't want to hear his voice or see him at all. By the way, he is an expert liar and faker. He can even make himself cry on demand. I don't want anything to do with him. How about if I don't care whether he apologizes or not, because I don't care if he's dead or alive?

Stephanie: Speaking with my ex to see if he'll apologize seems like the opposite of detaching, and I thought that's what we're supposed to do. It sounds like enabling. I will not be his victim any more.

Renee: I agree. Detaching and getting involved in the apology game sound like contradictions.

Pat: You're right that waiting for an apology from an insincere narcissist will get you pulled back into his net. You don't owe him forgiveness. And also, as I said, these sociopaths have no barometer for emotions; apologizing or thinking they've done something wrong isn't even on their radar screen. New research suggests that telling an abusive spouse or partner you forgive them can be seen by the offending person as weakness on your part and acceptance of the bad behavior. It's like they think they got away with it, which gives them a good excuse to continue the bad behavior.

This research is presented in an article entitled "The Dark Side of Forgiveness," by James McNulty, found in "Personality and Social Psychology Bulletin." Another good resource is the book "How Can I Forgive You?" The authors say there are more choices beyond forgiving. They challenge the assumption that forgiveness is a panacea. Acceptance may be the better route for you. Acknowledge the evil and accept that it is no longer your problem anymore. You are not obligated to reconcile or forgive.

Stephanie: Now that sounds right to me. I feel like I "forgave" him hundreds of times and kept giving him chance after chance to get his act together and be a good husband and father. He just yelled and pushed me around more and more.

Renee: This new research sounds right to me too. Pat, you once told me some conditions, like depression, ADD, or bi-polar disorder, can be treated with therapy and medicines, But treatment can't turn a sex addicted narcissist who's also a pathological liar, a misogynist, and a sociopath into a good person who's safe to be around. I want to stay far away from my ex. Stupidly, I did give him a second chance after my brother died, and it turned out he was lying to me again and conniving to get some of the inheritance.

I also believe if there was justice, maybe there could be forgiveness. But there's no justice here. I recently listened to an amazing story on the radio about a father who forgave the man who murdered his daughter. I was shocked. But the murderer was in prison for life, and can never murder another person. My ex is divorced and has gone on with his life. There is no justice in that. I might feel differently if he was arrested for prostituting a woman, thrown into prison, and died from AIDS. That would be karma at work, because he couldn't hurt and exploit another woman, and I would finally be safe as well. I think the drumbeat to forgive everyone for everything ignores a fundamental element: the person must feel safe from the abuser because he's dead or in prison or a few thousand miles away.

Pat: I agree that it's best for you to stay away from him. There's little chance that he has transformed in any way.

Debbie, do you think your ex-husband's desperate situation has made you look at him differently? You've been divorcing and suing him for several years.

Debbie: Absolutely, yes. I think I talked to Greg because his life fell apart. Now I have no chance of recovering any money from him. He's broke and he has no one.

Renee: I want to save my forgiveness for a person who deserves it, is contrite, and will use every fiber of their being to not re-offend. My ex doesn't even know the difference between truth and lies, love and hate. Seriously, he actually told me once there is no difference! I want forgiveness to mean I could shake the other person's hand or at least be in the same room. But that isn't the case with my ex. Instead of forgiving and not forgetting, I want to just forget and put it all behind me.

I was doing pretty well before the loan mess. I would go weeks without thinking of him at all, and if I did, I could swat him away like a bug thanks to Pat. Now, I would love some amnesia potion.

Stephanie: My ex is also not worth forgiving. But… what about forgiving myself? I still find that's where I get stuck. My sons make me feel like I was selfish for getting a divorce because they're suffering about being poor. I tell them I love them and things will get better. I do what you tell me to do when they're being abusive to me, especially my younger son. I walk out of the room when he's being horrible, but then I cry.

Pat: Forgiving yourselves is hard. You still feel responsible for enabling your husbands and having children with a man who turned out to be a bad father and husband. However, your divorces were logical and healthy responses to abusive husbands. Stephanie, your sons don't understand that now, but I believe someday they will. They will see how courageous you were to finally stand up to your husband. Someday, the money issues won't seem so important. None of you easily or quickly made a decision to divorce. You all thought and hoped you'd be married for life. Forgiving yourselves is most important.

Renee: I still blame myself sometimes. But when I think like that, I try to focus on the present and future, so I can be a positive person and especially a positive mom. I pray I have enough time on earth to make amends for his abuse of women, the pain he caused to my children, and the harm he caused to our community.

Debbie: Make amends for him? Why?

Renee: No, I don't want to make amends for him. That's for him and his Maker and his conscience. I want to make amends for me being clueless and therefore letting him do so much damage.

Pat: You are on a more positive path now, Renee. Debbie, you feel you could and should forgive your ex, and you told him so. Time will tell if this was a cleansing act on your part. Forgiveness to Renee feels like outside pressure to forgive, but she doesn't feel the need or desire to forgive. All of you are well aware how your husbands manipulated you, so you should be wary, whatever you decide to do.

Stephanie: Right.

Pat: But I keep going back to reminding you to work on forgiving yourselves and moving on.

Stephanie: Okay, I'll work on forgiving myself. But not him.

Sharon: I don't have the time or energy right now to think about this.

Pat: That's understandable. It takes a long time to even broach this topic.

Reader: I never knew forgiveness could be so complicated. These women don't sound cold to me—they are emotional and compassionate. I wonder if they can ever fall in love again.

Not Ready to Make Nice (excerpt)
by the Dixie Chicks

Forgive, sounds good
Forget, I'm not sure I could
They say time heals everything
But I'm still waiting.

I'm through with doubt
There's nothing left for me to figure out
I've paid a price
And I'll keep paying.

I'm not ready to make nice
I'm not ready to back down
I'm still mad as hell and
I don't have time to go round and round and round
It's too late to make it right
I probably wouldn't if I could
'Cause I'm mad as hell
Can't bring myself to do what it is you think I should.

Session Fifty

Any Good Men Out There?

Pat: Hi, everyone. Stephanie, you recently asked me about dating, which is an important topic we haven't discussed so far. Can you repeat your question?

Stephanie: Yeah, I'm wondering about when a person like me might date again.

Debbie: Do you want to date again?

Stephanie: No, but I was out with some friends from work and a guy across the room wanted to buy me a drink. That hasn't happened in 18 years. I stammered, "No, thank you," to the waitress and refused the drink. A friend said I should have accepted it. I couldn't believe it. I don't want to be picked up at a bar, but in a way it made me feel good.

Renee: You're so pretty. You should expect attention.

Debbie: Next time say, "Yes."

Stephanie: I need more time. I don't know if I'm ready to trust men.

Pat: Stephanie, you were following your gut in a good way to refuse the drink offer. You aren't feeling ready to date. You will probably know if and when you're ready. I usually advise women to wait until they've been separated at least a year. And although most people don't want to hear this, I think it's best to wait a year post divorce, giving you time to settle into your new status as a single woman. You need time to know yourself again; to figure out your likes and dislikes. Then you'll be sure of what you want and need in a relationship.

Stephanie: Do any of you date at all?

Debbie: I've been out a couple of times, but I'm not focused on it.

Renee: I absolutely don't want to date.

Sharon: I know I'll date again someday, but for now I'm still trying to figure out how to live.

Pat: My best advice is to take your time.

Stephanie: I don't want to get into an abusive relationship ever again. I fell in love with my ex, so I'm worried it could happen again.

Pat: It can happen again, especially to women who feel they need a man to feel complete. It also can happen if you jump into a relationship too soon, before getting to know what you truly need and want. Before you date again, I recommend you know yourself and feel capable on your own.

Stephanie: Is there a magic wand I can wave over a man to see if he's a good person?

Pat: Alas, there is no magic wand. But you can learn to see with "eyes wide open" regarding how a man treats you. Lots of good men are out there—you just need to become more perceptive and realistic in finding them. I often say in therapy that I think you truly don't know anyone until you've gone through all four seasons of a year. You may think you do after a month or two, but I believe anyone can fake it for a month or two, or even six months. After six months the warts of every person start emerging, and by a full year you have a better gauge of what the guy is like.

That's another reason I recommend taking time before you date again, because you spend four seasons getting to know yourself. After that, you're stabilized from the divorce and ready to move forward and date. I often tell clients to please come and talk things out with me when they meet a guy they're getting serious about. At times I've even met some of these guys to see what they're like.

Stephanie: Well, I'm definitely going to take you up on that offer.

Sharon: Me, too, for sure!

Reader: I like the idea about taking your time to readjust after divorce before dating. But, what if you don't want to date or marry again, ever?

Session Fifty-One

Choosing a Single Life

Pat: Renee, you seem adamant that you don't want to get married again. Why is that?

Renee: The last thing I would do with the rest of my life is get married. Whether I live one more day or several decades, I want to recover myself and live in peace.

Pat: Do you mean recover yourself or recover from the divorce?

Renee: Both.

Pat: So you want to recover from the abuse and heartache, as well as discover and uncover who you truly are? You want to recover yourself as a human being who was happy and content before meeting and marrying your ex. Is that right?

Renee: Yeah. I spent my marriage trying to figure out how to please my husband, and I seldom thought about myself. Year by year, he chipped away at me and I became more and more silent. I barely recognized myself after 28 years of marriage. It was hard to face the fact that while I convinced myself I was a flexible, modern wife, who was not demanding. I was really enabling him to do as he pleased. Now I want to develop my interests and work for causes that mean a lot to me. This will include plenty of friends, but no dating.

Stephanie: I think I'll date again someday and maybe fall in love. I'm not a man hater.

Renee: I never want to be married again, but Stephanie, I'm not a man hater because I hate the man I was once married to. Some of my best friends are men. I love my brothers-in-law and dearly loved my deceased brother.

Stephanie: I didn't mean to say it that way.

Debbie: Renee, what do you want to do?

Renee: I have kids and work and my siblings. Soon I'll retire and volunteer more. I'd like to live a purposeful life and make amends to this community for enabling my ex to exploit and hurt so many women. I found out about some organizations that help people escape from being trafficked and others who work with women who were battered.

Debbie: I'll do more volunteering also.

Sharon: I'd like to date again someday, but now I need to concentrate on my kids. I definitely don't hate men, but I am wary.

Stephanie: My sons are out almost every night. When I'm home alone I get depressed. I plan to sell the house and the bad memories as soon as I can.

Pat: The words "I want to do this" and "I want to do that" are music to my ears, no matter what tune you decide to play. You are playing your own instruments now, and you are fabulous.

Reader: I have so loved being with these women. Will the group continue forever?

How does Divorce Feel?

I sleep alone soundly
I cook for one simply
I clean the house happily
I love my kids completely
I plant my garden joyfully
I think my thoughts calmly.
I wear the clothes that I choose
I go for walks where I choose
I watch what I choose and I read what I choose.
I am poorer, but worth more.
I feel worthwhile contentedly.

–Renee

Session Fifty-Two

Who Am I Now? Becoming Your Complete Self

Pat: Hi everyone. Since we don't have any big issues to discuss tonight, let's reflect on how far you've come and who you are now—after divorce, individual therapy, and so many group sessions.

Stephanie: I want to be the person I was before I met him.

Sharon: Me too. I wish I could rewind the last ten years of my life. I used to be a confident, accomplished person. I can barely believe I got myself into such a bad marriage.

Pat: What makes you happy now?

Sharon: My kids. I'm so happy I have my two children and I'm learning to be a good single mom for them. For now, they are the center of my universe. I also want to be just me, not the woman who's divorced. I want to be Sharon, a college grad who traveled a lot, worked in publishing, and has two sweet children.

Pat: What makes you happy, Stephanie?

Stephanie: My kids. They give me the most joy because they're so great. But they also give me the most pain when they treat me the way their father treated me. I think we have a lot of work to do as a family.

Pat: I agree. Keep going to counseling and I urge you to try Al Anon. What about you, Renee?

Renee: After tons of individual therapy and coming to this group too, I can say that I've learned a lot. It's strange how learning in school was easy for me, but when it came to dealing with my husband, I had to learn everything the hard way. From now on, I'll try to steer clear of liars, narcissistic sociopaths, and creeps. Life is too short and precious to deal with bad people. For me, I want to be a good mom and become myself again.

Pat: Debbie?

Debbie: I want to stay as positive as possible. My kids are my world, and they need me to be a complete person, not preoccupied with divorce and litigation. I want to show them my love is steady and reliable for them. And it is.

Sharon: I also know it's important to be grateful for my friends, neighbors, and especially my mom for all their help. My mom has been indispensable.

Pat: Sharon, you have a good role model in your mom for a strong, resourceful woman. You're fortunate to have her.

Stephanie: And I am grateful to all of you who propped me up for the last year.

Renee: We help each other. I was already divorced when I first met Stephanie and Sharon, but I needed other women to talk with about what happened. I know my friends and family were concerned for me, but I can't vent to them about private details like I can here. You were a good reality check for me. So thanks all of you!

Debbie: Yes. I have felt supported, and I hope I was helpful in group.

Stephanie: Yes, definitely.

Sharon: Group helped me a lot.

Debbie: Pat, you asked who we are now. I want to stand on the roof of my house and shout "I'm a survivor!" There are marches for cancer survivors. I wish we could march for women who divorce liars, cheats, and creeps.

Renee: You have definitely survived!

Debbie: Now I can think about my future. Before the divorce I thought the rest of my life would be just like it had been for years. Yech. The hardest part of divorce was feeling like I was standing on a cliff not knowing how the future would be. That was scary at first, but now I like the feeling. I am unshackled from an alcoholic man who was dragging me down. I never want to be pulled down again.

Pat: This is another time for me to remind you how skilled your husbands were at manipulating and controlling you and a lot of other people. They robbed you of your individuality for a period of time, but you were ultimately strong and brave. You all survived difficult marriages and divorces. Now is the time to move past surviving into starting new lives and thriving. I wish you all well!

Reader: I think I'm going to cry. I am so proud of all these great women.

Face It

I face it,
my past.
I see it, but
I reject its hold.
I rebuild myself.
My Self.
With face wise wrinkled
and eyes wide bright,
surfacing now to be
Face to face with myself
and being in this moment.

–Renee

Epilogue

Anniversary Session

Pat: It's good to see you all tonight. I don't know if you realize this, but we've been meeting as a support group for a full year. Fifty-two weeks of love and sharing. I feel blessed and honored to be part of the journey with all of you. At this time we need to decide if we want to continue as a support group, and then choose how often we will meet. Who wants to start this discussion?

Sharon: I feel like I'm just getting my feet on the ground and I definitely want to keep the group going. I need the support I get each week from each of you.

Stephanie: I know I want to continue. I still have stress with my teenage sons.

Renee: I'd like to keep going, too. I feel pretty well on my way, but I want to help other women who are starting this journey. I don't need to meet weekly anymore, but maybe we could meet once a month.

Debbie: I love the group, but my life is changing, and I plan to be doing a lot more traveling. Therefore, I think I'm ready to say "adios" for a while. I'd love to have everyone's email so I can stay in touch with you that way.

Renee: We'll miss you, Debbie, and your direct, spot-on advice. I'd love to share email addresses and keep in touch.

Sharon: Me too.

Stephanie: I want to stay in touch.

Pat: Thanks, everyone for your input. We will miss your humor, Debbie, and your passion for justice. I understand it's time for you to get on with your life and new ventures. I wish you well. The rest of you sound eager to continue, and I'm more than happy to continue facilitating the group. Actually, I have a new client who expressed interest in joining the support group. I wanted to talk to you about her and see if you're okay with having her join.

Renee: I think it's good to have new members. Tell us what you can about her.

Pat: Frannie said I could share some details with you. She is a forty-four year old woman, married twenty years to Sam, her college sweetheart. They have two pre-teen children. Frannie found out a couple years ago that Sam had multiple one night stands while away on business trips, and then discovered he'd fallen in love with a woman he had an affair with for six months. Frannie originally told him to leave the house. After a seven month separation, they reconciled and decided to stay in the marriage. Sam swore he wouldn't cheat on her again.

But, a big problem remains: Sam's binge drinking. When he drinks he says he blacks out and can't remember anything he does. Frannie worries that he'll cheat again when he's out drinking with his buddies. She's in a codependent relationship with him and tries to rein him in all the time so she can make sure he doesn't get drunk, or that he only drinks when she's around. When I told Frannie about a support group with other women whose husbands have cheated and had problems with alcohol, she was excited to meet all of you. So what do you think? Does she sound like someone you'd like to add to our group?

Sharon: I'd like to have Frannie as a new member. She sounds like someone I can relate to.

Stephanie: I agree. Just speaking for me, I'd like another group member who's dealing with an alcoholic. Even though we're divorced, I still have to deal with my ex's drinking.

Renee: I would be happy with a new member, and Frannie sounds like someone who could use our support whether she decides to stay in her marriage or not.

Pat: Great! Then I'll invite Frannie to attend our next meeting. How about we meet in a month and see how that works for us on a monthly basis?

Sharon and Stephanie: That sounds great.

Pat: Since this is the one year anniversary of group, perhaps each of you will share something about where you see yourself now after a year in group therapy, and what you hope for in the future.

Renee: Okay. I am here, that's the biggest thing. For four years, I wasn't at all sure I'd survive. I know life won't be easy going forward, and I also know I can't control anything or any person other than myself. I want to live quietly and with purpose. I want to be a good mother to my grown children. I want them to see me at my best, not my worst.

Debbie: I want to live a purposeful life, and I want my kids to see me devoted to them and making a difference in our community. I hope to get more involved with my church and work on women's issues. I will also travel a bit to see the wider world. I spent too much time focused on my bad marriage and the divorce. I also hope my ex and I, now that he's starting in AA, can manage to have a better relationship related to our children.

Sharon: I want to feel safe again, laugh, and be silly with my kids. I love them so much. I wish I could make them un-see the bad stuff that happened in our house, but I can't. So I'll make sure they see me being a strong woman and mom, and maybe someday they will see me in a healthy relationship.

Stephanie: I need to look for a better paying job, sell my house, and find another place to live. I'll try to do everything you said about walking out of the room if my sons say abusive things to me. I want them to become good men. I promise to find out when Al Anon meets. That's all I can handle for now.

Pat: Thank you all so much for sharing. You are all remarkable women, and have come far over this past year. And so here you are now: Four women who've been through bad marriages and difficult divorces, supporting each other and making it to today, wishing what happened to you never happens to another woman. You will continue to get better, healthier, and safer every day, and you will continue to help each other and "pay it forward" to other women who enter our circle of support. Thank you for being here for each other!

Reader: I have a lot of thinking to do. At least I know I'm not alone in my feelings. I will keep this book nearby and start asking for help from a therapist or support group. Now I know that getting help isn't a sign of weakness; it's a sign of strength.

Afterword

Sharing Stories: The Value of Group Therapy

PERHAPS the stories from these four magnificent women started you thinking about the similarities and differences in their lives, and how their stories are like yours. As I worked with each of these women in individual therapy, I heard from every one of them, "I feel so alone. I can't believe I'm stuck in this situation."

Some of them went on to say, "I'm so capable and adept at my business dealings—how can I be such a mess in my personal life? Something must be wrong with me."

I repeatedly tried to reassure each woman that she wasn't alone and was certainly not stupid. Too trusting, perhaps, but not stupid. "And anyway," I'd continue, "Why shouldn't you be trusting? You're supposed to be able to trust your spouse."

No matter how much I tried to restore confidence in these women, my words seemed to fall on deaf ears, until my "Aha!" moment! I would start a support group so they could share their stores and realize they weren't alone. And voila! The group began.

What a journey we've had. We travelled through each other's lives. We shared joy and struggles, and we have all survived through our empathy and support for each other. We can be crying one week and laughing the next, but always respectful of each other's efforts and struggles, and we banded together to offer support and empathy.

The power of group therapy comes from the willingness of each member to trust the group and share. In sharing stories, including the painful pieces, each group member is freed to disclose her life's difficulties. Our willingness to be vulnerable and share our flaws, weaknesses, and struggles, gives others in the group permission to reveal and be honest as well. As blogger and author Carol Christ wrote:

"When one woman puts her experiences into words, another woman who has kept silent, afraid of what others will think, can find validation. And when the second woman says aloud, 'Yes, that was my experience too,' the first woman loses some of her fear."

The group provides an opportunity for the member and the group leader to be educated and informed by the experiences of others. It is a time to obtain hope for the future from members who faced the same struggles. Group members experience a sense of being nurtured and supported in ways that are different from individual therapy. The members often support each other outside the group by staying in touch throughout the week. They will go to court with a group member or offer encouragement through the struggles of leaving an abusive relationship.

The Group Leader

The success of the group is partly influenced by the group leader's expertise, confidence and style. As a therapist, I think it best to consider yourself part of the group. Being willing to share personal experiences and struggles can be useful to the group, although this must be done with thoughtful awareness of what will be useful to the women. The group leaders should also ensure that every member has a chance to share and group sessions aren't routinely dominated by one or two members. An occasional session will focus on a member who's having a particularly difficult time, but this is done rarely and with the consent of every member.

Each group participant knows the day may come when she needs to have the spotlight.

One of my favorite authors, Irvin D. Yalom, a psychiatrist, wrote an influential book, *The Theory and Practice of Group Psychotherapy*. He explains the power and curative nature of the group by the altruistic caring of each member. He uses the following allegory to express the altruism and effectiveness of group therapy:

An old Hasidic story tells of a Rabbi who had a conversation with the Lord about Heaven and Hell. "I will show you Hell," said the Lord. He led the Rabbi into a room In the middle of which was a big, round table. The people sitting at the table looked famished and desperate. In the middle of the table sat a large pot of stew, enough and more for everyone. The stew smelled delicious and made the Rabbi's mouth water. The people round the table each held a spoon with a long handle. Each one could reach the pot and take a spoonful of stew, but because the handle of his spoon was longer than a man's arm, he couldn't get the food back in his mouth. The Rabbi saw their suffering was terrible.

"Now I will show you heaven," said the Lord, and they went into another room, exactly the same as the first, with an identical round table and pot of stew. As before, the people were equipped with long-handled spoons—but here they were well nourished and plump, laughing and talking. At first the Rabbi didn't understand.

"It's simple, but requires a certain skill," said the Lord. "You see they learn to feed each other."

As our group forges on, we welcome new members, and continue to feed each other through our common purpose of survival and leading a healthy life after leaving an abusive relationship. May we all continue to thrive and let our self-esteem evolve so that we become channels of love and instruments of change toward social justice for all those who are suffering in relationships of abuse and domination.

Power and Control

Definitions of Domestic Abuse

Physical Abuse

Inflicting or attempting to inflict physical injury and/or illness, e.g. grabbing, pinching, shoving, slapping, hitting, hair pulling, biting, arm twisting, kicking, punching, hitting with blunt objects, stabbing, shooting.

Withholding access to resources necessary to maintain health, e.g. medication, medical care, wheelchair, food or fluids, sleep, hygienic assistance. Forcing alcohol and/or other substance abuse.

Sexual Abuse

Coercing or attempting to coerce any sexual contact without consent, e.g. marital rape; acquaintance rape; forced sex after physical beating; attacks on the sexual parts of the body; bestiality; forced prostitution, unprotected sex, fondling, sodomy, sex with others, use of pornography.

Attempts to undermine a person's sexuality, e.g. treating one in a sexually derogatory manner, criticizing sexual performance and desirability. Also, accusations of infidelity, withholding sex.

Psychological Abuse

Instilling or attempting to instill fear, e.g. intimidation, threatening physical harm to self, victim and/or others, threatening to harm and/or kidnap children, menacing, blackmail, harassment, destruction of pets and property, mind games.

Isolating or attempting to isolate one from friends, family, school and/or work, e.g. withholding access to phone and/or transportation, undermining one's personal relationships, harassing others , constant "checking up," constant accompaniment, use of unfounded accusations, forced imprisonment.

Economic Abuse

Making or attempting to make a person financially dependent, e.g. maintaining total control over financial resources including victim's earned income or resources received through public assistance or social security, withholding money and/or access to money, forbidding attendance at school, forbidding employment, on-the-job harassment, requiring accountability and justification for all money spent, forced welfare fraud, withholding information about family finances, running up bills for which the victim is responsible for payment.

> ## Emotional Abuse
>
> **Undermining or attempting to undermine a person's sense of self-worth,** e.g. constant criticism, belittling one's abilities and competency, name calling, insults, put-downs, silent treatment, manipulating another's feelings and emotions particularly inducing guilt, subverting a partner's relationship with the children, repeatedly making and breaking promises.

Adapted from: Domestic Abuse Intervention Project, Duluth, MN, (Copyright 1999 by the New York State Office for the Prevention of Domestic Violence)

Resources

Books

American Psychiatric Association, *Desk Reference to the Diagnostic Criteria from the DSM-5*, Washington, D.C., American Psychiatric Publishing, 2013.

Beattle, Melody, *Codependent No More: How to Stop Controlling Others and Start Caring for Yourself*, New York: Harper Collins, Hazeldon Foundation, 1987.

Hare, Robert, *Without Conscience: The Disturbing World of the Psychopaths Among Us*, New York: Guilford Press, 1999.

Maltz, Wendy and Maltz, Larry, *The Porn Trap*, New York, Harper Collins, 2008.

Norwood, Robin. *Women Who Love too Much: When You Keep Wishing and Hoping He'll Change*. New York: Pocket Books, 1990.

Spring, Janice Abrahams, *How Can I Forgive You? The Courage to Forgive, The Freedom Not To*, New York: William Morrow Publisher, 2005.

Stout, Martha, *The Sociopath Next Door*, New York: Broadway Books, 2005.

Van Der Kolk, Bessel, *The Body Keeps Score*, New York: Penguin Group, 2014.

Yalom, Irvin D., *The Theory and Practice of Group Psychotherapy*, New York: Basic Books, 1975.

Articles

McNulty, J.K. "The dark side of forgiveness: The tendency to forgive predicts continued psychological and physical aggression in marriage," *Personality and Social Psychology Bulletin,* 2011, 37, p. 770-783.

Organizations

Alcoholism: www.aa.org,

www.alanon.org

www.12steps.org.

Codependents of Sexual Addicts: www.cosa-recovery.org

Sexual Addiction: www.sexaa.org

Book Club Discussion Questions

1. Do you think the book's conversational format succeeded?

2. Do you know any women who've been in situations similar to any of the members?

3. Why is it so hard to break up a relationship with men like these ex-husbands?

4. Were you surprised these women took over a year deciding to divorce?

5. Did you find the section on diagnoses from Pat helpful?

6. Do you recognize people in your own life who fit one of these diagnoses?

7. Do you think any of these marriages had a chance to survive in a healthy manner?

8. What do you think these mothers need to do to raise healthy children after the divorce?

9. How do you think you could warn another woman to avoid dating/marrying a sociopath?

10. What is the value of therapy?

11. What is the value of a support group like this?

12. Do you think these women will now have better lives?

Notes

Acknowledgements

From Renee

I am deeply grateful to Dr. Martin for being my life raft through the tsunami of a painful divorce. Without Pat's patient guidance and brilliant insight, I would not have survived to co-write this book. I also thank my loving children who make me so proud; my dear siblings and their spouses, and the friends who stood by me and steadied me through tumultuous times; my skillful attorneys; and the strong women of the support group for their encouragement and permission to join me in telling their stories to help other women.

Our hope In writing *Liars, Cheats, and Creeps* is to instruct that domestic abuse, whether physical, emotional or psychological, can happen to any woman, at any age, at any income, and regardless of IQ or level of education. Any women can be fooled by liars, cheats, and creeps. We also hope to illuminate the problems that women in abusive relationships face on a daily basis, and to inspire and assist these women to choose a different life for themselves and their children—a life free of abuse and full of love and purpose.

–Renee Forte

From Patricia

It was quite an exhilarating, "woohoo" moment when we sent our final edited manuscript to our publisher. Renee and I have had quite the journey together writing this book. We have become dear friends and have supported each other through many uphill climbs and downhill thrilling rides. So first and foremost, thank you to my writing buddy!

And next on the list of people to acknowledge are our steadfast editor and publishers, Sammie and Dee Justesen. We feel so fortunate to work with Norlights Press and thank our lucky stars (pun intended) to have such wonderful guidance along the way. I also thank Erin Chrusciel Photography for the author cover photo; she made me look better than I could ever imagine; and Kate, who suggested the inspired and spot on title, *Liars, Cheats and Creeps*.

We are grateful to all the women in the support group who so willingly and eagerly allowed us to write their stories in this book. Their enthusiastic response of "YES," was often followed by, "and I think our therapy group will help other women." Their generosity of spirit is truly appreciated.

Also, sincere thanks to all the many clients I've had the pleasure to work with over my thirty plus years of practicing clinical psychology. I am particularly grateful to the remarkable women I counseled who have the courage and conviction to leave abusive relationships and begin lives as empowered, free women. You are truly inspirations for me. I have grown in wisdom and compassion because of you.

Although *Liars, Cheats, and Creeps* focuses on abusive, sociopathic men who have tormented thousands of women over the centuries, I must acknowledge the world of wonderful men I've had the honor to know throughout my life.

First, I credit my wonderful father, Edward J. Peters, as my model for what a good man should be. His passing three years ago was one of my most difficult losses, but his lessons live on in each and every one of his five children and fourteen grandchildren. Dad, you and Mom taught me well, and because of you I chose an extraordinary man to be my partner and friend throughout life. Jim, you are my true companion! I thank my three wonderful daughters who are selecting good men as mates, and my son James, who makes me proud every day with his kindness and thoughtful, caring ways. Finally, I want to acknowledge the many loyal, dedicated men who are virtuous and committed to living a faithful life of devotion to family and friends. Good men abound; let us not forget that.

–Patricia P. Martin, Ph.D.

ABOUT THE AUTHORS

Patricia Peters Martin, Ph.D., is a Phi Beta Kappa graduate of Georgetown University and holds a doctorate in clinical psychology from Purdue University. She is co-author of *The Other Couch: Discovering Women's Wisdom in Therapy.* Dr. Martin makes frequent appearances as a commentator on the local public television affiliate and is a guest columnist for a large metropolitan daily and its online affiliate.

Dr. Martin has done research work at the National Institute of Mental Health studying bi-polar disorder, and at the National Institute of Child Health and Human Development studying the effects of early environment on child development. She has taught and supervised graduate and undergraduate psychology students at Purdue University, Springfield College, and Bay Path University. She has counseled thousands of clients in her 35 years of clinical practice in New England and the Midwest. Her patient population includes children and families, individual adults, and teenagers and couples.

During her career, Dr. Martin has worked with thousands of women who were traumatized by domestic abuse and she facilitates therapy groups with women who've been in abusive relationships. She has been married 37 years and is the mother of four children, the grandmother of three, and lives with her husband in western Massachusetts.

271

Renee Forte is a pen name for the coauthor of *Liars, Cheats, and Creeps*. This author chose a pen name to protect the identities of her wonderful children, who are innocent victims of a marriage that should never have been. The name Renee Forte translates to "Re-born Strong."

Renee is a summa cum laude graduate of college and a member of Phi Beta Kappa, with a master's degree from a professional school and a long list of professional certifications and volunteer activities. She sought therapy from Dr. Martin who said these words to her during the first appointment: "I can help. You will get through this."

Patricia Peters Martin, Ph.D.

CPSIA information can be obtained
at www.ICGtesting.com
Printed in the USA
LVOW04s2026181016
509271LV00011B/1222/P